POLITICAL DEVELOPMENT THEORY

AUTHORITY
E.D. Watt

FEDERALISM AND FEDERATION
Preston King

POLITICAL DEVELOPMENT THEORY
Richard A. Higgott

THE HISTORY OF IDEAS
Edited by Preston King

THE CONCEPT OF HUMAN RIGHTS
Jack Donnelly

THEORIES OF INDUSTRIAL SOCIETY
Richard Badham

Political Development Theory

THE CONTEMPORARY DEBATE

Richard A. Higgott

CROOM HELM
London & Sydney

© 1983 Richard A. Higgott
Croom Helm Ltd, Provident House, Burrell Row,
Beckenham, Kent BR3 1AT
Croom Helm Australia Pty Ltd, Suite 4, 6th Floor,
64-76 Kippax Street, Surry Hills, NSW 2010, Australia
Reprinted 1986

British Library Cataloguing in Publication Data

Higgott, Richard A.
    Political development theory.– (Croom Helm
    international series in social and political
    thought)
    1. Underdeveloped areas – Politics and government
    I. Title
    320.9172'4   JF60

    ISBN 0-7099-1252-8
    ISBN 0-7099-1257-9 Pbk

Printed and bound in Great Britain by
Biddles Ltd, Guildford and King's Lynn

CONTENTS

For my Mother and Father

PREFACE AND ACKNOWLEDGEMENTS

Writing intellectual history, or even more modest historiographical analysis, is an ambitious and presumptuous activity. It is also probably the kind of activity best pursued in the later rather than the early stages of an academic career. Indeed, when I started on the project, it was never intended to be a book. On commencing to teach courses in political development five years ago, I was struck by how difficult it was to get across to students the vast gap between the two dominant perspectives on political and social change in the Third World. In fact, it was quite embarrassing to try to explain why scholars, looking at the same problem areas, could adopt such different descriptive and pre-scriptive positions. Most of the students were too inquisitive to be fobbed off with the suggestion that it was simply alternative 'ideologies' or 'world views' — although that is certainly a part of the answer. I was not prepared simply to teach what *I* perceived as the 'truth' and to write off the other perspective as ideology. To do so would have been both presumptuous and intellectually dishonest. Apart from that, I was never sufficiently sold on the total superiority of the one approach to allow me to reject *in toto* the other. Since I would not resolve the matter by suggesting to students that 'truth' lay somewhere between our two dominant modes of thinking, I was in a somewhat uncomfort-able position.

I set out, therefore, to write a series of lectures on the historical development of both schools of thought. There was a vast body of secondary literature. It was not difficult to put each school of thought into some kind of socio-historical perspective — to detail the variety of contemporary thinkers, their ideas, and the impact they had had on the study of political development in the post-World War II period. Having once outlined the components of the two schools of thought, however, it all seemed a somewhat unsatisfactory exercise. On the one hand, it still did not *explain* why these schools had developed in the manner they had; on the other hand, it also seemed that one should really go further than simple narrative and offer a few suggestions as to future developments. This book is then a brief attempt — it could have been much longer — to explain the bifurcated nature of the study of political development. It is also an attempt, not to suggest a possible synthesis, of the two dominant modes of thinking under review, but, much more modestly, to suggest areas of common ground on which both modes can forage for the benefit of each other.

Numerous people have helped in a variety of ways in the production of this book. As editor of the series in which this volume appears, Preston King provided all the right kinds of prodding and comment at exactly the times they were needed. John Ballard of the Australian National University; Cherry Gertzel, Richard Leaver and Bill Brugger of Flinders University; and Robert Curry of California State University at Sacramento all provided valuable comments on my work — without of course carrying responsibility for the finished product. In particular Don Rothchild of the University of California at Davis commented in invaluable fashion on the work in both its initial and final stages. In addition, his gentlemanly and friendly response to my somewhat gauche and immature critique of his and Robert Curry's *Scarcity, Choice and Public Policy in Middle Africa* stopped me in my tracks and caused me to rethink considerably my own intellectual position. His response more than anything else caused me to see the importance of moving beyond my initial negative attitude towards the public policy of development literature. Don's criticisms of my early work sent me in search of the common ground on which I hope public policy approaches to development and radical theory can, and will, cooperate. While I have still used *Scarcity, Choice and Public Policy in Middle Africa* to illustrate, at times in critical manner, the intellectual metamorphosis of political development theory, I would like to acknowledge the work's importance in trying to pioneer, for all the right reasons, the public policy of development.

The first draft of this book was produced whilst I was teaching political development at the University of Western Australia in Perth. Whilst this is a beautiful part of the world, it is remote from the intellectual centres of development studies. The final draft of the manuscript was produced whilst I held a Fulbright post-doctoral research fellowship in the John F. Kennedy School of Government at Harvard University. This piece of biographical data is important. Harvard, and MIT, were the intellectual home of the Social Science Research Council's Committee on Comparative Politics, which was to be the major influence on the political science of political development. When I first decided to prepare this project for publication, I was concerned that my understanding of the intellectual evolution of political development was based almost exclusively on a reading of the major texts and critiques. I knew nothing of the *dramatis personae* and their environment and assumed this could only put me at a disadvantage. My period in the USA helped to resolve my doubts.

On reflection, I am of the opinion that the primary consideration in the production of historiographical analysis must be the actual texts concerned. In this regard, I owe thanks to three fairly important post-World War II students of political development — James Coleman and Richard Sklar of UCLA and Bob Packenham of Stanford University — with whom I discussed my work somewhat timorously in their first instance. Whilst they too are in no way responsible for anything I have written, their enthusiasm for the project reassured me I was at least on the right track.

Finally, I would like to thank Leonard and Cornelia Wheeler, Gordon and Shirley Clark and Penelope Greene for providing shelter and friendship in Cambridge, Mass., whilst I completed the book, and my wife Anne for constantly reminding me that there is more to life than political science.

R.A.H.

INTRODUCTION

In many ways the study of developing countries has been, to coin a popular phrase, the 'cutting edge' of post-World War II social and political theory. This is particularly so if we accept the view that teaching and research in the social sciences tend to reflect the prevailing interests and priorities of the wider society. Consequently, and despite early expectations, disillusionment with the performance of the Third World (in more than one sense) has steadily increased since the period of heady optimism which abounded in the late 1950s and early 1960s. The expectation of the problem-solving social scientist that it was possible to plan for prosperity in the Third World, and that most of the problems were primarily technical in nature, was to be short-lived as problems not only endured, but in many cases increased, throughout the first United Nations Development Decade of the 1960s.

If nowadays most people agree on the symptoms of underdevelopment, fewer agree on the cause. During the 1960s and 1970s the nature of the disagreement tended to polarise around two loose schools of thought which, because of their ideological overtones, have tended to be seen as mutually exclusive of one another. The broad and largely ill-defined nature of these schools — which can loosely be referred to at this stage as the *modernisation school* and the *radical school*[1] — has tended to do severe harm to the complexity, and the subsequent study, of development and underdevelopment. Further, emphasis on 'competing ideological perspectives', 'competing paradigms', 'bourgeois and radical' schools etc. has meant that there has been little effort to see them together. The tendency has been to assume that the two schools are mutually exclusive and then to go on to operate in one camp or the other depending on ideological, intellectual and methodological predilections.

To a certain extent, of course, they are mutually exclusive; but in other ways, to be explained in this monograph, they exhibit a remarkable amount of similar characteristics, especially when looking at their intellectual origins on a thematic basis. Partial synthesis, in some circumstances, might be in order, but it is not the intention of this monograph to present such a synthesis. Such an approach more often than not leads to what one author has called 'meaningless togetherness' (Sartori 1970: 1052). Rather, the purpose of this monograph is to try to demonstrate the development of the *study* of development and underdevelopment. Attention will focus not only on the differences between competing philosophies, and the differences which exist *within* philosophies, it will also highlight the similarities that overlap the two major schools of thought which have to date dominated development studies. From such a base it is the intention to suggest that the study of development, going into the 1980s, is a good deal more complex than was initially, and commonly, assumed.

Such an exercise can best be carried out in the context of an intellectual history grounded in a methodology strongly influenced by the sociology of knowledge. As such, this monograph is not an exercise in the analysis of the problems of development and underdevelopment *per se*. It needs rather to be seen as an exercise in the development of recent Western social and political theory. 'Theory' is used in the broadest sense. There is no theory of development in the formal sense of hypotheses which have been verified in systematic manner through empirical study. Further, the monograph contains little detailed discussion of the social, economic or political conditions prevailing in the Third World today. Such descriptions abound nowadays, and a reading of this work assumes a basic working knowledge of 'development studies'.

There is a body of knowledge about social and political change which, historically speaking, can most suitably be seen as ideas about progress, development and evolution. These ideas, more often than not used indiscriminately and interchangeably, are part and parcel of the intellectual history of Western social and political thought. To attempt to date the origins of such ideas would be impertinent, and involve us unquestionably in a discussion of all thought from Greco-Roman times and beyond.[2] This monograph is concerned more or less exclusively with the post-World War II period and the application of these ideas to the *study* of developing countries. Suffice it here to allude to the influence on this post-World War II body of literature of the social and political thought dating from the time of Europe's industrial revolution and the transformation of thinking from an essentially religio-superstitious view of the 'way the world works' to a view which emphasises the importance of science, technology and rationality. The period following the industrial revolution has witnessed the growth of a 'social science' which is the logical outcome of the scientific and technological revolutions which have preceded and accompanied it. This suggestion still holds good even if we accept Alvin Gouldner's very persuasive suggestion that there was a binary fission in Western social thought in the middle of the nineteenth century between Marxism and its derivatives on the one hand and a 'positivist' social science parented by Auguste Comte on the other (see Gouldner 1970). Scientific method was to be every bit as important to the 'scientific socialists' as it was to be to the positivists. We have, however, because of their different prescriptive end-states — as supporters of either capitalism or socialism — tended to ignore the epistemological similarities of both positivist and Marxist social science (see Hyden 1980: 245). If we accept, largely unchallenged at this stage, the importance of these intellectual beginnings for post-World War II modernisation theory and radical development theory, this book will demonstrate the similarity of their epistemologies as highlighted, for example, in the defence of their respective positions against a common intellectual enemy — the dependency theory of the late 1960s and early 1970s.

To sum up, this book provides an account of theories about development as reflected in the largely academic literature of the last couple of decades. It is only secondarily, i.e. as it influences our historiography, an analysis of the success or otherwise of the developmental process in the Third World. To those who would suggest the enterprise is largely an exercise in academic/intellectual navel-gazing I plead guilty. In mitigation, however, I would make two points. First, and for better or worse, the academic study of development and underdevelopment in the West is perforce largely dominated by theoretical concerns — for reasons I will suggest in Chapter 1. Second, and whether we like it or not, the theoretical corpus of knowledge operating within the Third World, as Paul Streeten (1974) has pointed out, is still primarily externally provided. The suggestion of Chapter 1 of this book concerning the major role that theory plays in the study of the Third World is a description of reality: it is not intended to be supportive of the way things are.

It is possible that we are at one of those junctures in political and intellectual history that cries out for the brilliant theoretical innovator with a talent for creative synthesis. In certain respects the time seems ripe for going beyond the rigid established ideologies and paradigms and establishing more fruitful and compelling new ones. But if the latter-day Hobbes or Locke or Rousseau or Marx lurks in the historical wings, he is not yet discernible. Failing the advent of such a comprehensive theoretical innnovator, we shall have to make do with messy approximations of partial truths (Packenham 1973: 357).

1 DEVELOPMENT AND THE SOCIAL SCIENCES: A SUGGESTED FORM OF ANALYSIS

Since World War II, all theorising about political development, be it positivist or Marxist, has in many ways emphasised 'thought' at the expense of material life. Ideas were taken to be the creator or determinant of the form history was to take in the Third World. It was commonly believed that the problems of the Third World could be solved by directly applying theoretical constructs derived from the study of the historical evolution of the West. When Western social, economic and political theorists turned their attention to the problems of the decolonising and developing world in the wake of World War II, the social, economic and political changes they came to expect — whether higher levels of economic productivity, rationalisation or secularisation — were widely accepted as deriving from our rapidly increasing knowledge of the world, both physical and social (see, *inter alia*, Black 1967: 7; Eisenstadt 1973: 231 and Boulding 1965: 27-53).

If we consider the central theoretical concerns of 'development studies' in the post-World War II period loosely as 'growth', 'modernisation', 'progress', 'development' or whatever, then it has to be said at the outset that the academy has fared much better than the actual focus of its attention — namely, the developing countries themselves. If the growth and development of the Third World had mirrored the growth and development of its chroniclers and theoretical analysts (in the 1960s especially), the Third World would now be a much healthier place. The contemporary decline of development studies is less to be explained by the 'take-off', or not as the case may be, of the Third World, than by the limited accomplishments, both theoretical and practical, of development theory itself.

The assumption of a decline of development theory is not to be concluded from any perceptible decrease in the *volume* of literature on development issues, but rather from the lack of any substantive beneficial impact of this literature on the problem area to which it is addressed. We are in a period of pessimism in which any kind of synthesis and progress beyond the work of the last two decades or so seems unlikely. New and innovative ideas seem hard to come by and developments in theorising over the last decade are largely the result of a return to older and more tried theories — or variations thereof. Particularly influential have been efforts to re-adapt both Marxist and

1

liberal classical theories to the problems concerned. The malaise in development studies is in large part due to a growing acceptance that the likelihood of 'solutions' to our problems are extremely remote. Many bold reformist solutions would appear largely unacceptable in an increasingly conservative, cut-throat, hostile and perceived zero-sum international economic and political environment.

It is not intended to suggest there have been no advances in theory-building over the last decade. Indeed there has been advance, but it has put us further back from out initial starting point. We now recognise that problems are much more intractable than when we first set out to solve them in the late 1950s and early 1960s — that optimistic period of the decolonisation process and the commencement of the UN Development Decade. Our initial theoretical assumptions were simply not a reflection of Third World reality, be it at a domestic level or the level of the Third World's position in the international economic and political environment. Our major advance is that descriptively we are much further on in understanding Third World political and economic reality. Our major weakness is that, as a consequence of this increase in comprehension, we are *prescriptively* further back than we were when we started theorising about development after World War II. Our recognition of the complexity of development and under-development means that we have inevitably lowered our sights. Knowing that many questions fall quite simply into a 'too-hard box', we now, especially as far as policy-making is concerned, ask questions which are much less ambitious.

While development studies are extremely heterogeneous, transcending a variety of disciplines, they were all at the outset charged with the same post-World War II optimism, which asserted the mutually beneficial nature of the relationship between the developed and the developing worlds and the possibility of the transference of theoretical knowledge from the former to the latter. Such an ideological support system justified not only the political decolonisation process but, underwritten by the intellectual genius of Western socio-technological knowledge, the appropriateness and virtuousness of the transplantation of Western culture, institutions and technology. I trust the reader will not consider it too cynical to suggest that had we been aware of the magnitude of the problem, and the real feebleness of our theoretical weapons to cope with them, then that altruism that we have seen might not have been as substantial as it in fact was. Development studies had their birth in the boom period of post-war reconstruction in the northern hemisphere — not a period of dire economic crisis, accompanied by a belief in the zero-sum, non-mutuality of the relationship between developed and developing countries in the international system that prevails in the current climate at the beginning of the 1980s. Nowadays there has been a clear shift from the middle ground that was occupied in the early phases of post-World War II development by Keynesian welfare-inspired developers. Put briefly, we have on one side of the middle ground the neo-classical right, epitomised in the critique of interventionist policies by authors such as Peter Bauer (1976 and 1981) and analysts of what Robert Cox has called the 'Establishment' perspective (Cox 1979). On the left, we have a resurgent Marxist analysis. There is of course a basic irony in the fact that the lines of criticism developed by the Establishment and Marxist scholars of the radical structuralist and dependencia theorists of underdevelopment, despite different ideological perspectives, are basically the same.

Methodological Issues

Perhaps the major factor that has become apparent over the last couple of decades is that there is no such thing as a 'typical developing' country. Methodologically we have to be extremely careful about trying to aggregate data, knowledge and ideas about the Third World. The literature of the 1950s and 1960s assumed a homogeneity in the Third World which led to generalisation of such a nature, in both schools under review, as to lead to a distortion of reality. Perhaps the prime example at this stage was modernisation theory's fetish for the tradition— modernity dichotomy (see Price 1975).

Theory-building really does have to pay serious attention to the problems of generalising about the conditions and prospects of states as diverse as Brazil, Argentina, Taiwan or Nigeria on the one hand, and states such as Bangladesh or the Sahelian states of West Africa, such as Mali, Upper Volta or Chad on the other. In the past, theory-building based on polar opposites — be it Weberian ideal types or radical attempts to provide explanations of underdevelopment by generalising from André Gunder Frank's early and near ubiquitous metropolis— satellite polarisation — has meant that little or no account has been taken until recently of regional, spatial or temporal disparities. The danger of such polar analysis is that reality tends to become subordinate to theory. On the other hand, it can be argued, as Scarrow (1969: 33) does, that 'generalisations are the hallmark of all scientific endeavour' and that generalisations must therefore be made. The brief of this book — to provide an overview of the recent intellectual history of development theory — must permit such a generalising approach.

We accept that macro-sociological concepts can hide much of the socio-economic reality of the Third World, just as the aggregation of statistics and data can hide the failure of development theory actually to improve the lot of *people* in the Third World; and just as focusing at the level of the nation, or even the region, ignores much of the political, social and economic activity which takes place at the level of the smaller unit.

Several other initial methodological problems that have beset the study of underdevelopment by social scientists need to be raised at this stage. First, the tendency towards specialisation. While the academic heritages of the sociologist and the social anthropologist are important, neither is entirely sufficient in its own right; the same can be, and is of course, said about the specialised material of the economist and the political scientist. Even given the realities of academic differentiation and, at a less savoury level, the rivalries of academic professionalism, a multi disciplinary approach should not be entirely beyond our means. The major problem is in dealing with a situation in which solutions cannot be presumed to emerge simply from aggregating the various disciplines of the social sciences:

> The fundamental problem . . . is that the social sciences are linked by a common subject matter rather than a common theory — where disciplines operate in generally different fields but are linked by a common theoretical base (as say, biochemistry and mechanical engineering depend on a common stock of ideas about molecular and atomic structure) the problem of joint application is much less than where the disciplines operate in the same field but with different intellectual bases (for example biochemistry and psychiatry) (Cumper 1973: 248).

A second problem is to be found in the relationship between the social sciences and society. More than any other branch of the academy, social scientists reflect the conditions under which their work emerges; while society is the object of study, it does at the same time, to a greater or lesser extent, determine the direction inquiries will take. Working from such an assumption, it will be argued throughout this monograph that the various phases of development studies very largely reflect the prevailing moods of optimism, pessimism, resignation and even cynicism that have characterised certain stages in the study of underdevelopment.

In trying to write this intellectual history it has become clear that new ideas on development theory (and probably new ideas in general) would appear to go through three phases. First, a stage of organised resistance and hostility to a set of ideas as the old view comes under challenge. Second, a stage which sees a largely uncritical support and acceptance of these new ideas when they are deemed to have 'arrived'. Third, a stage, which is practically and intellectually the most reward-ing, in which the new perspective undergoes a period of critical evaluat-tion. Chapters 2 and 3 will try to illustrate that this progression in stages has taken place in post-World War II development theory.

The first stage can be characterised as one of growing criticism of modernisation theory as the initial optimism of the 1950s and early 1960s began to fade and a sustained critique of the theory was developed. The second stage, the late 1960s and early 1970s, can be characterised by the rise of a crude radical alternative in the work of early Latin American dependency theorists and its uncritical acceptance in many areas. The third stage, from about 1974, has to date seen a critical evaluation of notions of dependency, from both left and right, resulting in an increasingly sophisticated debate about the nature and causes of underdevelopment. This stage exhibits two main facets: first, a stimulating, if at times convoluted, neo-Marxist debate over the nature of class formation and the role of the post-colonial state in the Third World, to be discussed in Chapter 3; and second, the resurgence of liberal theory as 'post-conventional' development theory, to be discussed in Chapter 4.

The utility of such a review will lie not in its originality, but in its attempt to treat the recent intellectual history of development theory *as a whole*. There are many individual studies of orthodox and radical theory, but few studies which try to see them in relation to each other through various phases of intellectual development.

To talk of 'phases' of development is not, however, to imply that this progression should be seen as some kind of Kuhnian paradigm change. While there is indeed some kind of dialectical relationship between competing schools of thought, they have in other ways developed 'internally' and quite separately from each other's influ-ences. Chapter 2, for example, argues that the response to the crisis in modernisation theory has not been to plump for the radical alternative of the neo-Marxist but to restructure itself from within. Remaining largely within their North American intellectual tradition, and in keep-ing with the responses to the inadequacies of behaviouralism, political scientists, for example, have placed a growing emphasis on political economy — not the political economy of the neo-Marxist, but a political economy using rational-choice models, and decision-making and policy-analysis approaches, to the study of political behaviour in the Third World.

Similarly, as Chapter 3 argues, radical theory, without having as pure a parentage as modernisation theory, and despite its initial flirtation with the radical structuralism of early Frankian dependency theory, is developing more and more into a debate about the rectitude or otherwise of what are seen as variants of *internal* neo-Marxian analysis. Both schools of thought would appear to be running along parallel lines having little *direct* influence on one another.

It is, therefore, important that we consider briefly in this introduction the tendency, exhibited by several authors of late, to apply Kuhnian 'notions' of theory development to the study of underdevelopment. 'Notions' is used loosely since these authors represent only a small percentage of the social scientists who have watered down and popularised Kuhn's concepts in order to justify a proliferation of paradigms in the social sciences (Perry 1977).

Susanne Bodenheimer (1971), for example, developed an ideological critique of modernisation theory which she termed the 'American paradigm surrogate for Latin American studies'. Aidan Foster-Carter (1976) used Kuhn's ideas in a self-explanatory paper entitled 'From Rostow to Gunder Frank: Conflicting Paradigms in the Analysis of Underdevelopment', and Raymond Duvall (1978) argued that concepts of *dependence* and *dependencia* were paradigmatic in as much as they represented distinct conceptual views and epistemological underpinnings. Such work clearly illustrates the currency of Kuhn's views, for better or worse, amongst students of development and underdevelopment and suggests that there is a need at this stage to consider their relevance or otherwise.

Perhaps a first point worth noting, and more or less universally accepted, is Kuhn's view that the social sciences are in a pre-paradigm situation. The study of development or underdevelopment is clearly not established science in the Kuhnian sense; as will be seen, neither of our schools of thought has established an ascendancy which would allow for a process of normal and revolutionary science.

Perhaps more relevant to the kind of historiographical analysis provided in this book is Imre Lakatos' notion of a 'research programme' (Lakatos and Musgrave 1970), as opposed to the more commonplace Kuhnian paradigm. As one author has suggested, albeit in another context, such a concept allows us 'to steer a middle course between the scylla of Kuhnian relativism and the charybdis of positivist formalism'

(Ball 1976: 152). A utilisation of the ideas of Kuhn and Lakatos in combination helps us to see that changes in paradigms, pre-paradigm theories, research programmes or simply theoretical orthodoxies are, as often as not, as much sociological as methodological processes.

Borrowing from Lakatos, this book will, by examining the dura-bility of modernisation theory and broadly defined 'Marxist' theory, suggest that neither theoretical approach has been killed off (or falsi-fied) in empirical fashion. As research programmes, for analysing devel-oping countries, both modernisation theory and Marxism would appear to be made of sterner stuff. They are 'good swimmers' that have sur-vived in an ocean of anomalies. Both research programmes have at times seemed at risk, as testing has appeared to be 'degenerative' or 'content decreasing' (Ball 1976: 165) — especially during the hey-day of depend-ency theory in the late 1960s and early 1970s. The last few years, however, as this book attempts to show, have demonstrated that both theories are extremely durable. Neither is likely to disappear from development studies in the foreseeable future. This is because both research programmes have a greater degree of validity than either is normally prepared to concede to the other and also, for slightly more negative reasons of the kind alluded to by Ball in his study of behavioural political science, 'no matter how waterlogged it is a research program will not sink and have to be abandoned until a better, more buoyant one comes along to replace it' (Ball 1976: 165-6).

While modernisation theory and Marxism have both come under attack as research programmes, neither has seen its fortunes plummet in the manner of early dependency theory. In their different spheres, both modernisation theory and Marxism are fairly strong and, as will become apparent, this is in large part due to their shared view, albeit from con-flicting normative positions and in sharp contrast to dependency theory, of the essentially progressive nature of capitalism in the Third World. This common progressivist core has kept these competing re-search programmes afloat amongst a variety of ephemeral fads and fantasies. It is because of the similarity and strength of this common core that one needs to avoid what Lakatos has called 'dogmatic falsifi-cationism'.

Historiographical analysis demonstrates the essential durability of the hard core of both modernisation and Marxist approaches and suggests the need for a greater 'tolerance in matters theoretical' (Ball 1976: 171). Rather then engage in dogmatic falsification, we need to allow much greater latitude to research programmes in a subject as young as development studies. As I will try to suggest in the conclusion to this work, maybe our two competing schools should not be so auto-matically contemptuous of one another as they have tended to be in the past. Historiographical analysis, by a process of reconstruction, also helps explain the kinds of adjustments that take place in the protective surrounds of a theory's inner theoretical core.

The modifications that have been imposed upon the initial Hobsonian/ Leninist theories of imperialism by dependency theorists such as André Gunder Frank, Paul Baran and later world systems theorists like Immanuel Wallerstein and Samir Amin, represent a perfect case study for this form of analysis. This process is given full treatment in Chapter 3. Similarly, our historiographical analysis of modernisation theory in Chapter 2 enables us to highlight major modifications in the research programme. Such a methodology closes for us the unreal gap that emerged in the later 1950s and early 1960s between normative and empirical social and political theory. Attempts to minimise the norma-tive component are no longer deemed feasible or acceptable in the 1980s as they were in the hey-day of attempts to create a value-free social science in the early 1960s.

The broad conclusion that emerges from historiographical analysis of the *study* of developing countries is that, despite the critiques of their respective research programmes, concepts like modernisation and imperialism are indispensable to any meaningful analysis. Such a con-clusion must suggest that the essence of these research programmes is therefore basically sound. No social or political theory can ever attain widespread and long-lasting support without it containing an element of truth, and consequently important social theories never disappear in their entirety (see Grew 1980). Rather, the essence that does 'seem true' tends to reappear in reformulated pattern, as I intend to suggest with regard to both modernisation theory and, for example, variations on a theory of imperialism.

Historiographical analysis is in essence a component of the sociology of knowledge. Adopting a sociology of knowledge approach, rather than some kind of Popperian positivism as a way of understanding post-World War II development theory, gives a more important weighting to the influence of environmental factors on a particular intellectual view-point at a particular point in time. As Sheldon Wolin has written:

> many of the great theories of the past arose in response to a crisis in the world, not in the community of theorists. It was a methodo-logical breakdown that prompted Plato to commit himself to the *bios thereotikos* ... it was ... the ... breakdown of the Athenian

polis. . . There is no need to multiply the instances: the paradigms of Machiavelli, Bodin, Hobbes, Locke, Tocqueville, and Marx were produced by a profound belief that the world had become deranged (Wolin 1968: 147-8).

The study of development and underdevelopment needs to be seen from such a sociological perspective. For example, the development theory of the 1950s and 1960s (modernisation theory), perhaps more than any other branch of the social sciences, grew out of an idealistic hope for some kind of brave new world. These hopes were accompanied by the belief that advancing technology and a benign capitalist system could not but overtake and benefit the Third World. Similarly, there was faith that the political institutions of liberal democracy could and should be imparted to the Third World.

In contrast, the growing influence of radical theory in the late 1960s and early 1970s gained credence in the light of the crisis of American liberalism. Characterised by pessimism, the late 1960s saw an acknowledgement of the failure of Third World societies to approximate, in real terms, to what had been expected of them in theoretical terms. When coupled with American involvement in Vietnam, this mood of pessimism was to see a severe questioning of early modernisation theory. Indeed, for many young social and political scientists:

opposition to the war was often the start of a more profound and difficult shift in intellectual orientation rooted in an increasing discontent with the scientific inadequacy as well as unacknowledged ideological preconceptions of liberal development theory (Berman 1978: 208).

Berman's words would seem to resound with the sense of 'conversion' (Kuhn 1970: 151) that accompanies the rejection of one paradigm — even though a new paradigm is by no means clearly outlined or providing any proof that it will be superior to the old. With hindsight, however, it will be argued in Chapter 3 that a new paradigm, in most senses of Kuhn's view, was not provided in the writings of early radical theorists operating in a Frankian dependency mould. Further, despite a substantial growth of support for a 'radical' alternative to modernisation theory, there has not been a wholesale migration of scholars from an orthodox to a radical school of development theory.

It is consequently the contention of this monograph that the current debate on development cannot be seen as a paradigm shift. Not only has there been no major defection of liberals but, as Chapter 3 will show, there are major problems in recognising a 'neo-Marxist paradigm' — despite Aidan Foster-Carter's (1976 and 1973) admonitions to the contrary. Notwithstanding their common Western intellectual origins and their undoubted secondary influence on each other, our two major schools of thought need to be considered as independent, but Western, intellectual traditions, each preoccupied with their own problems and internal dialogues. There is an added danger that emerges from this situation that needs noting; to see development theory in a paradigmatic manner is to minimise the great complexity and divergence of the two schools. We need, therefore, when making points about the discontinuous nature of scientific growth, to take care that we do not understate not only the divergence but also the elements of continuity within and between competing schools.

The kind of historiographical approach adopted in this book allows us to pin-point quite firmly the major continuities and discontinuities in the development of development theory. If, therefore, we subscribe to the notion of a 'research programme' or a paradigm at the basic level of a framework which provides direction and organisation to an area of investigation, then it can be of utility in understanding theory development. Indeed, in an intellectual history such as this it is vital to recognise that

> no scientist sees paradigmatic bundles of ideas carried around like mental baggage. He simply absorbs some ideas, and unless he reads Kuhn's book, he uses them without being aware of their collective impact as his perception and curiosity (Ricci 1977: 22).

It is from this point of view that the early work of Bodenheimer (1971) and Packenham (1973) was important for exposing us to the collective nature of the 'ideology of developmentalism' that underpinned modernisation theory. The recognition of the ideological mainsprings of radical theory does not present us with the same kinds of problems as did the recognition of the 'ideology of developmentalism'. In the recent tradition which Gouldner (1970) refers to as 'academic sociology', the sociology of knowledge pertaining to 'radical theory' has always been more sophisticated and openly self-critical that an 'auto' sociology of knowledge of the 'academic' school.

Two further methodological issues in relation to the general role of theory are still in need of some discussion. First, a historiographical analysis of development theory does not provide us with a traditional view of theory-building in which information is simplified and sifted until we are left with an essence providing understanding. Rather, it is more appropriate to perceive the post-World War II growth of development theory as a gradual 'encroachment' of ideas; that is a process of accretion of knowledge in which the scientific component, in a Popperian positivist sense, is subsidiary to the prevailing sociological climate, intellectual fashions and ideological needs. Second, we need to recognise a danger inherent in any study of the history of ideas – the tendency for the study to convey a greater sense of coherence and sequence to the ideas in question than often exists. It is for this reason that 'accretion' is possibly a more suitable description of the process of growth than 'development'. To talk of the development of development theory implies a process of explicit selection and rejection of aspects of theory on the basis of an organised set of criteria which simply is not supported by historiographical analysis. Post-World War II development theory is better seen as a set of responses to a series of stimuli such as, for example, the change from optimism to pessimism characteristic of the post-1960 period. Yet modernisation theory came under attack not because fact refuted theory – indeed, 'facts' of Third World development or underdevelopment were largely irrelevant to the normative and prescriptive aspects of modernisation theory – but rather because the old perspectives were out of tune with the growing belief in the late 1960s that the efforts of the social sciences to break free from the realm of the 'metaphysical' into that of the 'value free' had largely failed. From the other side of the glass, the growing popularity of 'radical' theory, in its initial guise of dependency theory, needs to be seen as a shift in intellectual orientation prompted not primarily by the scientific inadequacy of the previous dominant form, but by a growing acknowledgement of the unacceptability, at that point of time, of its widely acknowledged normative assumptions. Further, just as the decline of modernisation theory had little to do with the 'fit' of evidence, neither did a comparable 'fit' of evidence entirely explain the growing popularity of radical approaches in the late 1960s. With this background in mind, Chapters 2 and 3 of this book treat 'modernisation' theory and 'radical' theory in comparable fashion. Examination will focus on time phases, intellectual influences that predominated in these phases and the thematic innovations that have taken place within the post-World War II life of these schools. The principal foci of these chapters are, therefore, the nature and roots of *ideas* and *theories* about development and underdevelopment, not the nature of development and underdevelopment *per se*.

Considerations of space require that Chapter 2 restrict its coverage of modernisation theory. While recognising that modernisation theory represents in fact a combination of the social science disciplines — specifically economics, sociology, psychology and political science — Chapter 2 'isolates out' political science from the social sciences for particular consideration. This is done for several reasons. First, the political science of political development provides in its own right the necessary background to look at the wide intellectual origins and ideological underpinnings of modernisation theory in general. Second, political science provides a quite specific and clearly defined intellectual community and body of literature, virtually institutionalised by the American Social Science Research Council Committee on Comparative Politics, which makes itself amenable to cohesive treatment. Perhaps a third reason for focusing on political science is that the changes that have taken place within this particular discipline reflect what is perhaps the major trend of the social sciences over the last decade — namely a rediscovery of the importance of economics.

The study of development and underdevelopment as a 'cutting edge' of the social sciences has played no small part in the growing fashionability of political economy. Not the least of political economy's attracttions for orthodox development theorists, in the first instance, is the belief that it presents some kind of integrated alternative to the previously distinct social sciences. We might in fact suggest that the problems of the developing world have provoked an academic return of sorts to nineteenth-century political economy — prior to the beginnings of that process of social science compartmentalisation that Gouldner suggests took place a hundred or so years ago (Gouldner 1971 and also Garson 1978: 204). In no area of the study of developing countries is the economy any longer seen as an independent variable to be analysed separately from other socio-political or cultural variables.

While we might 'all be political economists now', the intention of this book is to demonstrate quite specifically that all political economists are not the same. First, all political economy must not be seen as opposed to liberal development theory in particular, nor to liberal theory in general. As Leaver points out, 'political economy has always been an impeccable liberal enterprise' (1978: 20). Further, radical political economy is not the converse of liberal social science and an analysis of the bifurcations that have taken place between 'variants' of political economy is vital to any understanding of its growing popularity. The intellectual origins of orthodox and radical political economy do, of course, overlap, but their recent thematic innovations provide the important grounds for distinguishing between them. As Chapters 2 and 3 argue, our two major schools can both quite legitimately claim to be pursuing 'research programmes' in the 'political economy' of development, yet still be operating from quite different assumptions.[3]

2 FROM MODERNISATION THEORY TO PUBLIC POLICY: CONTINUITY AND CHANGE IN THE POLITICAL SCIENCE OF POLITICAL DEVELOPMENT

It was argued in Chapter 1 that the study of underdevelopment has been marked by a polarisation into two broadly based schools of thought. Despite the recognised weakness of applying such dichotomous classifications, such an approach enables us to discuss not only those debates that exist between schools of thought, but also within those schools of thought and, perhaps more importantly, the processes of transformation that each school has undergone over time. What follows in this chapter, therefore, is an exposition and critique of the recent non-Marxist literature on the politics of development in an effort to establish the clear links that exist between modernisation theory of the 1960s and that work which throughout the 1970s has come to emphasise public choice and policy analysis in the broader context of a 'new political economy'. Sticking closely to the historiographical form of analysis outlined in Chapter 1, it will be argued that: (1) the research of the 1970s reflects á greater deal of continuity (both conceptual and methodological) with the earlier work than is often assumed, (2) efforts to incorporate or accommodate the early inadequacies of modernisation theory have not been successful, and (3) much of the recent literature raises substantial problems in its own right.

It is neither possible nor necessary to review modernisation theory here; its general characteristics, guides to primary sources in the field and critiques are to be found in numerous survey articles (Bernstein 1971; Frank 1971; Tipps 1973; Higgott 1978). Rather, the intent is to examine the recent literature of North American political science concerned with political development, no matter how the concept is defined. Such a focus allows us to trace the critiques, reactions and modifications to modernisation theory over the last two decades. Consequently, the first section of this chapter, borrowing on the work of Robert Packenham (1973) and Ronald Rogowski (1978), delimits a simple threefold classification of political science: legal formalism, behaviouralism and post-behaviouralism. The emphasis is on the second period and what is seen as its transformation into the third. For the

purpose of this discussion a further division is also required. The literature of political development, as an integral part of behavioural political
science, has been divided into two subsections: that produced between
the mid-1950s and the mid-1960s and between the mid-1960s and
1971.

The second section of the chapter focuses on the period after 1971,
the 'post-behavioural phase'. This phase is the dialectical outcome of
the antagonism of institutionalism and behaviouralism. It has seen
political science opting for a more empirical and more economistic
conception of political development, as well as adopting the terminology (so much in vogue throughout current political science) of policy
studies, in creating what I have called the 'public policy of development'.

The third section of the chapter establishes an initial, and admittedly
rudimentary, critique of this public policy of development. In it, several
factors are emphasised; the failure of policy-oriented research to highlight the ambiguities surrounding what precisely is meant by 'policy
science', 'policy analysis' and 'policy studies'; the role of 'policy
approaches' (my preferred term) that focus on choice models for Third
World decision-makers as a vehicle for power concentration and regime
maintenance (irrespective of the nature of the regime); the methodological insensitivity of much of the Third World policy literature, to
date, concerning the transference of Western/industrialised forms of
analysis to the non-industrial context — particularly the limited utility
of incremental decision-making; and the tendency of policy approaches
to play down the role of structural dependence in the international
economic environment as a primary factor in the political economy of
new states.

Political Science, Modernisation and Political Development

1954-64

During this period the study of political development was dominated
by the work of the United States Social Science Research Council's
Committee on Comparative Politics under the chairmanship of Gabriel
Almond between 1945 and 1963. The impact of this committee has
been widely acknowledged (Holt and Turner 1975; Milne 1972), and as
Robert Packenham has noted, Few formalised academic groups have so
thoroughly set the course of a segment of social science scholarship as
did this committee' (Packenham 1973: 225).

The establishment of the committee reflected the post-World War II optimism that the growth of a 'scientific' social science would form the basis for rational exercises in social engineering. By the 1950s there was a feeling in many quarters of the social science community that the major economic problems of industrial society were under control: absolute, if not relative, poverty was on the decline, unemployment was down to unprecedentedly low levels, and education and welfare were reducing overall inequalities in industrial society (see, for example, Seers 1972). Those problems that had not been overcome tended to be seen in technical terms and were to be solved by growing technological expertise. They were not seen as problems with overwhelming philosophical or normative implications. Instead, social scientists were turning their attention towards improving their technique.

These successes also needed to be seen in the context of the success of liberal democracy contrasted with the failure of Fascism in the war and the disrepute into which Marxism had fallen as a result of the excesses of Stalinism. Advanced industrial Western society was established as the good society to which the colonial peoples could be steered by a process of guidance and diffusion. This background is particularly important for the growth of the study of developing countries. It is against such a background that modernisation was seen as:

[that] process of change *towards* [my emphasis] those types of social, economic and political systems that have developed in Western Europe and North America from the seventeenth century to the nineteenth and then have spread to other European countries and in the nineteenth and twentieth centuries to the South American, Asian and African continents (Eisenstadt, 1966: 1).

Eisenstadt's words touch the essence of the *dichotomous* approach which was to be central to the work of all modernisation theorists. Borrowing from the work of nineteenth-century evolutionary theorists, they built up a scheme based on comparisons of ideal-typical variables of tradition and modernity.[4] That this was the case in political science is testified to by Gabriel Almond:

Our theory building and modelling first took on simple dichotomous form. Working from the classic formulations of Max Weber, Ferdinand Tonnies and Talcott Parsons . . . several innovative social scientists . . . constructed models of traditional and modern forms of society and polity (Almond *et al.* (eds.) 1973:1).

In short, what we saw was the growth of an essentially dichotomous approach to the study of political development, based on the work of nineteenth-century evolutionary theorists, and the comparison of the ideal-typical variables, tradition and modernity. In general terms, we may speak of the importance of sociological 'grand theory' (Almond 1970: 274-5) for the work of the SSRC Committee on Comparative Politics. Two further important influences on the literature of political development in this first phase have been what Packenham (1973) has called the 'American Liberal' ideology and what Bodenheimer (1971) has called the 'ideology of developmentalism'.

In practical terms, this intellectual background meant the growth, during the late 1950s and early 1960s, of a substantial body of literature on political development under the auspices of, or greatly influenced by, the Committee on Comparative Politics. There were three basic kinds of literature:

(1)   theoretically oriented case studies such as those of Apter on Ghana (1957), Coleman on Nigeria (1958) and Pye on Burma (1962);

(2)   the Princeton University Press volumes of the collected work of the Comparative Politics Committee on Political Development (LaPalombara 1963; Pye 1963; Ward and Rustow 1964; Coleman 1965; Pye and Verba 1965; LaPalombara and Weiner 1966) and the final volume in the series by Binder *et al.* (1971);

(3)   the generally more theoretical volumes in the Little Brown series, the most important of which were Almond and Verba (1963), Almond and Powell (1966) and Pye (1966).

This literature marked a clear break with that work which Packenham and others had referred to as legal-formalism. While the prescriptiveness of legal-formalism went unchallenged, the literature of behaviouralism represented a shift in methodology from legal and institutional to economic and socio-psychological variables (Packenham 1973: 200). The development of modernisation theory in the first phase of the behavioural era was thus seen, in its political guise, as a means of facilitating the establishing of liberal democracy in new states.

Political science's concentration on the movement towards liberal democracy represented only part of a more comprehensive modernisation theory, based on the tradition—modernity dichotomy, shared with the other social sciences. This dichotomy is based on a Weberian view of tradition as pre-state, pre-rational and pre-industrial. It was criticised soon after its earliest application. The belief, built on the optimism of the 1950s, that the transition from tradition to modernity is primarily a technical problem disappeared with the growing disillusionment over the actual performance of new states in the post-independence period. In the mid-1960s it was recognised that simplistic attempts to classify societies in terms of certain pattern variables is unacceptable as a form of analysis. Equally unacceptable was the assumption that the advance from tradition to modernity would be a simple unilinear progression. There have been numerous critiques of the ascribed unilinear and teleological nature of modernisation theory (Kothari 1968; Gusfield 1967; Bendix 1967). For the purpose of this chapter, however, perhaps the most significant impact was made by Samuel Huntington (1965). His critique marks the boundary for my discussion of the literature of political development in the 1960s. The literature after 1965 had a different intellectual emphasis from the optimistic, 'democracy'-oriented literature of the first period.

1965-71

Writing in the second half of the 1960s, Huntington's importance lay in his challenge to the prevailing idea of the unilinearity of modernisation theory and in his stress on those issues that had been played down by earlier writers, especially the *dislocations* that arise in the modernisation process. Defining political stability in the normative sense, as the absence of open conflict, Huntington saw political development as the growth of institutions competent to deal with the strains of social mobilisation and political participation. Huntington was among the earliest to reflect the change of emphasis from 'democracy' to 'order' during the mid-1960s — a shift of emphasis outlined by O'Brien (1972) in his now classic discussion of political development in the 1960s. In this work O'Brien provides a detailed discussion of the shift of emphasis from 'democracy' to 'order' as the primary normative concept of the literature of political development. He argues that this shift is portrayed in the changing complexion of the membership of the SSRC Committee on Comparative Politics, particularly the appointment of Lucien Pye to the chairmanship in 1963 and Huntington and Aristide Zolberg to the board in 1967. Pye, and to a lesser extent Huntington, were among the most important theoreticians of counter-insurgency techniques, and Huntington (1968) and Zolberg (1966) both wrote important works on political order in new states.

Despite the confused views of political development that predominated in the second half of the 1960s, the concept of order emerges as central to most of the literature. Ithiel de Sola Pool, in perhaps one of the most widely quoted of quotations, taps the core of this order-based literature:

> it is clear that order depends on somehow compelling newly mobilised strata to return to a measure of passivity and defeatism from which they have been aroused by the process of modernisation. At least temporarily, the maintenance of order requires a lowering of newly acquired expectations and levels of political activity (Pool 1967: 26).

Similar discussions of the relationship between order and political development are to be found in Apter (1965: 67), Halpern (1965), Weiner (1967: 2f), and Huntington (1968: 5-55). The order-based literature reflected the changing political reality of the two phases of the first UN Development Decade, and it contrasted the earlier optimism of scholars such as Almond with the 'pessimistic prescriptions' of his successors (O'Brien 1972: 357).

The work of the second phase achieved its apotheosis in the last theoretical volume to be published in the SSRC Committee on Comparative Politics series, *Crisis and Sequences in Political Development* (Binder *et al*. 1971). The importance of this work is that is effectively represented the cumulative wisdom of the committee, and it provided one of the major links between the second (behavioural) and third (post-behavioural) phases discussed in this book. The link with the second phase was its emphasis on order. The link with the third phase, as will be seen, was its emphasis on governmental capacity to respond to, or to suppress, certain demands. Political development was seen as a political system's ability to cope with five crises: legitimacy, identity, participation, penetration and distribution (Binder *et al*. 1971: 65). Governmental capacity referred specifically to governing elites, and crises were therefore seen from the perspective of threats to the position of those elites and the necessity of elites for the maintenance of order. This position was especially evident in the chapters on legitimacy by Pye, political participation by Weiner and penetration and governmental capacity by LaPalombara (see Binder *et al*. 1971: 141-273).

That such strategies as suggested in *Crises and Sequences* could be used by elites of the right *and* the left was of secondary consideration. More important was that, as one commentator has noted, 'the interest in order of those at the top is given a logical precedence over the interest in social justice of those below' (Sandbrook 1976: 80-181).

Crises and Sequences in Political Development articulates many of the themes expressed by Huntington (1968) regarding the capacity of governing elites to preserve order, especially when Huntington's views on order are compared with Binder's views on crisis management. Both authors demonstrate a divergence from a more traditional American social science which sees political order in terms of a Parsonian value consensus. In a review of Binder *et al.*, Kesselman (1973) argued that, in its desire to safeguard the position of ruling elites, the literature of political development had supported a view of order as the end, not the means, to the good society. In so doing, modernisation theory made no attempt to measure the costs involved in the preservation of order.

In short, modernisation theory in general and political development theory in particular were criticised for their ideological and ethno-centric character (Bernstein 1971), the inadequacies of the 'functional category' approach, and their focus on the Parsonian concept of order as dependent on value consensus. For the purpose of this chapter, however, two other criticisms should prove to be of greater importance. First, the modernisation theory of the 1960s paid only lip-service to the multi-disciplinary nature of the problems of development, especially the tendency of the sociologist and the political scientist towards ahistoricism (Kon 1975: 64-5) coupled with the tendency to ignore economics as a major variable in any equation:

> In no other field of sociological investigation have the disastrous consequences of the economic illiteracy of professional sociologists been so starkly revealed as in the 'sociology of development'. Those who suffered less from intellectual parochialism where economics was concerned made up for this, moreover, with a hearty disdain for history. Rostow's master metaphor which saw underdeveloped economies as so many aeroplanes waiting to 'take off' was seductive not least because it seemed to provide an alibi for disconnected historicism which typified studies of the social factor in economic growth (Oxaal *et al.* 1975: 1).

Second, modernisation theory failed to understand the extremely uneven distribution of wealth between the 'haves' and 'have nots' of world society. That is, modernisation theory could not account for the growing gap between countries of the advanced industrial West and the large majority of new states in the Third World (Pratt 1973: 88ff).

With the total pessimism that engulfed the latter years of the first Development Decade, modernisation theory came to be characterised as ideologically tainted, methodologically inadequate and, perhaps most importantly, policy ineffective.

The late 1960s saw also the growing *radical* critique of development studies which argued that the work of those, such as McClelland (1961) and Hagen (1962) stressing achievement motivation, Huntington stressing levels of institutionalisation and Binder *et al.* stressing the role of bureaucracy and government capabilities, was only marginally relevant to the study of underdevelopment when compared to the nature of international dependency relationships and the world capitalist system. If we can talk in broad terms about 'development studies', then we see modernisation theory in this period assuming a subordinate position in relation to the growth and acceptance of a more radical/ neo-Marxist literature flowing from such authors as Baran, Frank, Amin, Wallerstein, Kay and Leys, to be discussed in the next chapter. The second half of this chapter, however, wishes to argue that radical development theory has in fact had little influence on the political development theory which emanates from the mainstream of American political science. The response to criticism, especially on questions of method, has been to stay within the broader responses to the inadequacies of behaviouralism. Such a response, it will be argued, has manifested itself in a rather confused, but nevertheless observable, option for a mixture of rationalist politics, public choice and policy analysis which for classificatory purposes has been gathered under the collective rubric of a 'new political economy'.

Political Development in the 1970s: from Modernisation Theory to Public Policy

During the 1960s, political science failed to build a 'grand theory' of modernisation that could adequately address itself to the problems of the Third World, either as analysis and prescription or at the policy level. Not surprisingly, this has led to efforts to build more empirically based theory, pitched at a much lower level of abstraction. The effects of this situation were twofold. First, political scientists were exhorted to greater policy relevance in their work. This point was stressed by none other than David Easton in his 1969 APSA presidential address (1969: 1056-7). Second, in relation to method, it led to a rediscovery of the importance of economics: a strand of analysis which some (for example Gouldner 1971: 92-4) have argued has been treated as distinct from the other social sciences for over 150 years.

In the broadest sense, the rediscovery of economics by the political scientist can be seen in the growing importance of rationalist theory. In our narrower context it can be seen in the growth of a 'new political economy of development' which caught on during the early 1970s and which, since the late 1970s, has been evolving into a public policy approach.

I have argued in the first half of this chapter that 'political development' needs to be seen in the context of the dominant approaches of the day towards political science in general, and it so happens that such a tendency becomes evident in the 1970s. This primary tendency involves the growing use of rational-choice models in the analysis of political behaviour; the 1970s being an era which one author has referred to as political science's 'fourth great revolution of the past century' (Rogowski 1978: 296) and what another has referred to as the 'end-products of behavioural theory' (Blondel 1978: 119-26).

Given that the most important questions in politics are still of the 'who-gets-what-at-the-expense-of-whom' type, it is hardly surprising that an approach which stresses bargaining and choice should gain a degree of popularity in political science in a period which has been characterised by a drift from the sociological to the economic. Rogowski's work traces this drift or rather what he sees as a 'sharp turn' within the discipline and he argues that the theories of rationalists such as Downs, Olson, Arrow, Schelling, Boulding and others 'have become, if not received truth . . . [they] . . . at least present a challenge that no serious student can ignore' (Rogowski 1978: 297-8). Similarly, William Jenkins (1978), in a recent work that expands on the views of Elkin (1974) and Mitchell (1969), traces the growing use of economic concepts by political scientists. Of particular importance, according to Jenkins, are the inroads that have been made into public policy by public choice theory. This is seen as part of the growth of a 'new political economy', in which authors such as Wade and Curry, in their *Logic of Public Policy* (1970), attempt to develop 'a normative theory of public policy' (Jenkins 1978: 138).

What Wade and Curry advocate is no more significant than what they reject, namely a belief in the analytical utility of sociological and historical categories: 'An appreciation of contemporary political economy requires the temporary jettisoning of such categories . . . and . . . a relentless commitment to logical discipline' (Wade and Curry 1970: 3).

The rejection of a sociological emphasis needs to be seen in the wider context of the growing antipathy of political scientists, post 1970, to sociological grand theory. But the antipathy to historical analysis needs a somewhat different explanation. Like the behavioural period of the 1960s, the 'new political economy' has little use for history as an explanatory variable. It is this position which distinguishes it sharply from the political economy of the radical school which places heavy emphasis on history; especially in the context of underdevelopment where the influence of the colonial period is deemed to be paramount.

Despite several caveats to the contrary, notably Almond's claim to be 'taking the historical cure', little use has been made of historical analysis in the non-Marxist study of political development. Almond, along with two younger scholars (Almond, Mundt and Flanagan 1973), edited a collection of essays entitled *Crisis, Choice and Change: Historical Studies of Political Development.* Of particular importance was Almond's and Mundt's two introductory essays which acknowledged the importance and growing acceptance of rational-choice theories of politics. The substance of this work, which in fact received adverse reviews (see, for example, Barry 1977), is less important for this discussion than the position of the book in the overall picture of the study of political development. If Almond in the early 1960s was at the forefront of the expansion of the horizon of comparative politics to include sociological and anthropological conceptualisations, in the early 1970s he was again at the forefront of a fundamental change which saw the inclusion of conceptualisations based on rational choice. The importance of *Crisis, Choice and Change* as with much of the literature to be discussed in the following pages, is that it represents in many ways as much a continuation of, as a breakaway from, the earlier work of modernisation theory. Almond and others, such as David Apter, in fact fill the role of midwives in the transition from period two to period three in our discussion.

If the increasing rigour of the rational-choice models used by economists is one of the major reasons for their growing attraction to political scientists (Rogowski 1978: 298), the opposite side of the coin has been that economists have been looking anew to the work of political scientists. The growth of the role of the state, planning and other intrusions into the market has radically disrupted the predictive capabilities of traditional economic theory in the post-World War II period, with the consequence that we are taking politics to economics just as much as we are bringing economics to politics: 'For what the economists are saying is that to the extent that their subject matter is becoming more political, it is becoming less susceptible to scientific and formalistic methodologies' (Almond and Genco 1977: 516). More generally, the new political economy of the early 1970s needs to be seen as the half-way stage in the transition from modernisation theory to public policy.

The New Political Economy of Development

It needs to be noted at the outset that this new political economy bears little or no relationship to the recent 'political economy of *under*development'. The latter has grown out of the radical structuralism of the ECLA economists in the post-World War II period, the work of the *dependista* school that developed and refined the ECLA approach, and that of the more orthodox Marxists who have criticised it. This new political economy of development, on the other hand, is a result of the recognition by political scientists that they needed to substitute a sociological for an economic emphasis (Almond 1970: 287). Yet, the new political economy must not be categorised as post-liberal theory merely because it arose in response to the limitations of behavioural and liberal political theory. The point of this discussion is that this form of political economy falls clearly within the liberal intellectual tradition. Its economic origins can be traced to Ricardo, Smith, Mill and Marshall, as opposed to Marx or his successors. Its political orientation came directly from the work of the earlier students of political development.

Perhaps the most useful way to illustrate the reason for, and the nature of, the growth of the new political economy is to examine some representative works. Several books and articles written during the crucial transitional period of the late 1960s and early 1970s demonstrate not only the continuity with modernisation theory, but also the major changes.

Warren Uphoff and Norman Ilchman, who wrote *The Political Economy of Change* in 1969 and edited the *Political Economy of Development* in 1972, are, by training, political scientists, *not* economists. Moreover, they are political scientists who were disillusioned with the state of their own discipline. They described their first volume as a

> respectful protest against the present 'state of the arts' for studying developing nations and the policy choices leaders in such nations must take . . . it is a protest against the failure of scholars in the non-economic social sciences to transcend typologies and *ex post facto* analysis and fasten their attention upon the achievement and improvement of public purposes; it is also a protest against the failure of economists to understand their subject in its political environment (Ilchman and Uphoff 1969: vii-viii).

Their work reflected the growing belief of that period in the policy irrelevance of modernisation theory, on the one hand, and in the value of the formal modelling being done by economists with an interest in the Third World, such as Rostow (1960) and Kindleberger (1958), on the other. What Uphoff and Ilchman were effectively arguing was that modernisation theory in a broad sense, and political science in a specific sense, were incapable of problem solution and policy orientation because they adopted 'a perspective quite removed from the process of choice or the ramifications of concrete political activity. Macroanalytical approaches which view society in global terms, cannot handle choices made by the statesman and other political activists' (Ilchman and Uphoff 1969: 8).

Many of the objections of these two scholars are exactly those that were being expressed towards behaviouralism generally in the American political science community. It is possible to see in the work of Uphoff and Ilchman the changes that were to take place in the language of politics in this transitional period. The previously fashionable concepts of 'system', 'function' and the grand Parsonian terminology based on dichotomies were giving way to concepts like 'policy', 'decisions', 'choice' etc. In reacting to the 1960s, Uphoff and Ilchman were at the forefront of those scholars who accepted 'economics as the science of choice' and political economy as the analysis of the 'economic effects of political choices' and the 'political effect of economic decisions' (Uphoff and Ilchman 1972: 2-3).

That the issue of choice should emerge as central in this new political economy is not surprising in the light of the influence of the early modernisation theorists. The concept had been used in the literature of the mid-1960s without ever having been well articulated. In 1965, David Apter, in the *Politics of Modernization*, hinted at the need for 'improvement in the conditions of choice and the selection of the most satisfactory mechanisms of choice' (Apter 1965: 9-11). Similarly, in 1966 Gabriel Almond called for 'a search for rational choice models of political growth . . . which may make political theory more relevant to public policy' (Almond 1966: 877).

David Apter's work forms one of the most important links between our second and third phases. In a book written in 1971, *Choice and the Politics of Allocation*, he tied together our two most important themes, namely order and choice. The purpose of the book was: 'to identify systems of order that do not ,penalise development and patterns of development that do not jeopardise order . . . Our point of departure is choice' (Apter 1971: 6). By asking how order could be maintained while choice was expanded, Apter provided continuity between order-based modernisation theory and choice-based political economy. Like Uphoff and Ilchman, Apter contributed to the growth of a public policy of development in the latter half of the 1970s — especially in identifying and discussing the priorities (in the broadest sense) that governments in new states might set for themselves.

Public Policy and Development

Considerable ambiguity surrounds the terminology of policy analysis (Anderson 1975: 219), as much as surrounds the earlier concepts discussed in this chapter. Theorists with an interest in political development have tended to join the bandwagon without articulating what they mean by policy science, policy studies, policy analysis, policy process or public policy. In the study of developing countries, 'policy' has tended to be used in its broadest sense; that is, it refers as often to values and social consequences as to processes and choices. Further, 'policy' tends to be seen as synonymous with 'state activity' (Feldman 1978: 288-9). This makes the term particularly attractive to analysts of new states, since the state is deemed to play a predominant role in most of these societies.

As with the new political economy, the importance of public policy analysis (or the less contentious term, 'policy approach') is its contrast with the behavioural political science of the 1960s. The period of legal formalism emphasised the importance of the state and institutions; and the behavioural period emphasised the centrality of the political system and inputs such as political socialisation, political culture and belief systems — i.e. the socio-psychological environment of the political system to the exclusion of process and policy outputs (Heclo 1972: 87). The growing popularity of public policy represents, in many ways, the dialectical outcome of the antagonisms of institutionalism and behaviouralism in political science.

Policy analysis represents a substantial change of emphasis by political scientists in two ways: first, it shifts the focus of the 1960s from inputs to outputs; second, it shifts the focus from macro-politics of an analytic kind to micro-politics of an experiential and contextual kind (Anderson 1975: 222). It is a change of emphasis from the system within which politics operates to the strategy of and for political activity. To concentrate on strategy is to see public policy in a problem-solving and public-choice context as opposed to being a product of a particular political system. Despite this undoubtedly justified change of emphasis in patterns of thinking, it is possible to argue that portents of what was to come were to be found in the early work of political development. References to Harold Lasswell's ideas about a potential policy science,[5] although never really articulated in the context of political development, are to be found in Almond's 1960 Introduction to *The Politics of Developing Areas*.

The movement by political scientists to economic forms of analysis and the growing importance of policy analysis are, of course, closely related. Indeed, economics' long involvement with policy analysis helps to account for its status as the most advanced social science in terms of theory development. It is this greater rigour and the narrower emphasis on policy and choice that researchers such as Uphoff and Ilchman felt was badly needed to replace the abstractionism of the 1960s. The grand theory of the 1960s can be characterised as explanation covering a wide number of cases with low explanatory power; the new policy-oriented approaches of the 1970s are an attempt to provide a form of analysis which covers few cases with more effective explanatory power. Ilchman and Uphoff paved the way in the study of developing societies of adopting limited goals with the hopes of achieving a higher success ratio then their predecessors: 'Policy oriented social science [they argue] adopts levels and kinds of explanations that can be tested and verified as a consequence of public choice' (Uphoff and Ilchman 1972: 12). It is not intended to subject such views to close scrutiny just yet. Rather the important point to note is the way in which such approaches represent a clear response to modernisation theory's methodological assumptions.

So far I have talked only about the growth of policy studies generally. What I would like to suggest is that its application and development in new states is in fact several years behind its development for use in industrial societies. This is meant to be a comment on political science at this stage, not a comment on the possibility of the successful application of the policy sciences to the Third World, which is altogether another question, to be discussed further on in the text.

It has already been noted that it is difficult to specify what various authors see as policy analysis. There is considerable disagreement over its basic characteristics and the direction in which it would appear to be developing — contrast, for example, the competing perspectives of several recent chroniclers of the general field of policy analysis (Heclo, 1972; Rose 1973; Feldman 1978). Thus to try to pick out its influence in the study of development and underdevelopment is a tenuous exercise indeed. The potential problems are highlighted by one student of public policy who draws on 'political development' to provide a useful analogy.

> Indeed, considering their theoretical sophistication, one may doubt whether such a goal is practicable. The better the work done on policy studies the more open ended theoretically the field seems to be. This is not a new experience for social scientists interested in political and bureaucratic topics. In the comparative politics movement the drive towards the theory of political development proved in itself to be a fruitless exercise. Since the scope of policy studies is at least as large as the field of comparative politics the relevance of this experience should be clear (Smith 1977: 259).

In short, there is a commonality of problems facing researchers in the 1970s as there was in the 1950s and 1960s. Policy studies are extremely open-ended. Albert Hirschman, perhaps one of the leaders of policy analysis in the Third World, argues that to study public policy is in fact merely another way of emphasising the relationship of state, society and politics (Hirschman 1975) — a view I strongly support in Chapter 4.

My suggestion, therefore, that there has been a shift from modernisation theory in the 1960s towards a growing use of public policy approaches in the study of Third World states is based on a somewhat small, but nevertheless growing, body of evidence. The evidence so far has been of two kinds: first, broad statements about the general drift in the study of political science as a whole; second, specific statements about the fusion of economics and politics into what Ilchman and Uphoff have called a 'new political economy'. The rest of this chapter will discuss in more substantial form the actual growth of policy analysis in the Third World, drawing evidence from several important volumes that have appeared in the last couple of years. If the analysis is correct, then my contention is that literature of this genre will proliferate over the next few years. The line of attack in the remainder of this chapter will be twofold; first, to demonstrate the *continuity* of the recent literature with the literature of modernisation theory (most of the major *changes* have been by now fairly well established) and, second, to raise several questions with regard to the utility of the application of a policy analysis approach in non-industrial society.

Perhaps the work that best illustrates both the continuity and change in question is the second edition of Gabriel Almond and Bingham

Powell's *Comparative Politics* (1978). The first edition (1966) was subtitled *A Developmental Approach*; significantly, the second edition is subtitled *System, Process and Policy*. Further, this completely revised edition contains a new final section entitled 'Public Policy' which includes a long chapter on the 'Political Economy of Development'. These changes, in what was one of the most influential political science books of the 1960s, reflect, in the authors' own words,

> an intellectual growth. In the first edition we stressed sociological, anthropological and psychological modes of analysis... In the second edition we elaborate our treatment of public policy. Our discussion of public policy and its consequences leads us to adopt a political economy approach (Almond and Powell 1978: vi).

Also important for the theme of this chapter is the recently published *Scarcity, Choice and Public Policy in Middle Africa* by Donald Rothchild, a political scientist with extensive African experience, and Robert L. Curry, the previously discussed economist who has written widely in the area of public policy theory (Wade and Curry 1970). This work represents one of the most concerted efforts to date to apply a policy-oriented approach to political behaviour in the Third World. The authors argue in favour of the new political economy which, given its emphasis on choice in relation to political and economic resources, can provide analytical insights into resource mobilisation and resource allocation.

They capture the 'essence' of the new political economy beautifully in the introduction to their book. They see such an approach as:

> an appropriate analytical tool to deal with the dynamics of social change that require the formulation and ranking of priorities and the developing and implementing of policy alternatives... Policy analysis combines two critical disciplines that are central to the process of transformation occurring throughout Africa today — political science and economics (Rothchild and Curry 1978: 4-5).

The emphasis of a policy approach in non-industrial societies relates primarily to problem-solving, management and maintenance, but within a limited context. Gone is the false optimism of the late 1950s and early 1960s. But despite the emphasis on relevance which appears to contrast sharply with the work of the 1960s, there is a high degree of continuity with the literature of modernisation theory. This must affect the way in which the new public policy approaches to developing countries should be perceived.

Old Products, New Labels?

The links between modernisation theory and public policy can be clearly seen in Rothchild and Curry's work in several ways. First, they draw heavily on the previously discussed Binder volume of the Committee on Comparative Politics Series, especially its identification of six 'crises' of political development 'which must be successfully dealt with for a society to become a modern nation state'. While acknowledging the ethnocentric nature of modernisation theory and delimiting some of the other inadequacies already discussed, Rothchild and Curry argue that 'modernisation theory presents a guide to our immediate concerns with setting systems goals in most African circumstances' (Rothchild and Curry 1978: 95). However, they go on to offer an important refinement to modernisation theory, in an obvious attempt to take account of the external factors in underdevelopment with which modernisation theory is incapable of coping. They suggest two more 'crises' that should be built into the crisis model. These are: 'the survival of the nation as constituted at independence; and securing freedom from external control' (Rothchild and Curry 1978: 95).

It is instructive and supportive of one of the major contentions of this chapter that, in discussing the external factors in underdevelopment, Rothchild and Curry do not refer to the radical literature on international dependency relations of the late 1960s and early 1970s. Instead, they turn to the work of that section of the American political science community which, in a behavioural mould, had been trying to create a scientific approach to the study of international politics, particularly to the work of James Rosenau and his notions of a 'penetrated political system' (Rosenau 1971). By a neat process of transformation, Rothchild and Curry turn the 'crises' of political development into a set of six key systems goals or 'collective tasks' for decision-makers: ensuring survival; establishing a national identity; integrating society; creating an acceptable authority system; mobilising and distributing resources; and securing freedom from external control. From these tasks, Rothchild and Curry then go on to produce a threefold classification of strategies for obtaining these goals: accommodation, reorganisation and transformation.

Rothchild and Curry's approach has been outlined in some detail because, I contend, it is not really a new approach; in fact, much of it can be found in the work of earlier modernisation theorists. The accommodation and reorganisation strategies on the one hand, and the transformation strategy on the other, bear a striking resemblance to David Apter's reconciliation-system/mobilisation-system classification (Apter 1965: Chs. 10 and 11) and James Coleman's and Carl Rosberg's pragmatic-pluralist versus revolutionary-centralising classification (Coleman and Rosberg 1966; Rosberg 1963).

The questions posed by Rosberg in 1963, as the basis of the mobilisation/reconciliation distinction, related to three characteristics of states: (1) the nature and mode of legitimation of authority; (2) the nature of the distribution of power within the community (especially the ruling party); and (3) the values, goals and problem-solving capabilities of the system — particularly with regard to the gap between the aspirations for rapid modernisation and the limited resources available to achieve it (Rosberg 1963). With certain refinements, the questions posed by Rothchild and Curry in 1978 are the same as those posed by Rosberg in 1963. A similar situation prevails with the answers to those questions, in theory if not in practice. Rosberg (1963: 32-45) provides a checklist of characteristics of mobilisation and reconciliation systems which could, without too much difficulty, be superimposed on Rothchild and Curry's (1978: 114) classification. For the purpose of this discussion, most important is the direct link that can be made between the work of the two periods.

To be fair to Rothchild and Curry, their classification is an advance to the extent that it is not merely a typology but also a guideline for various strategies of choice. At least this is the case as long as such choices are to be made by existing decision-makers to obtain some kind of optimum deal for their states. As Rothchild and Curry point out, the model they propose is predicated on the assumption that decisions are being made on behalf of all the citizens and not solely in the interests of the ruling, decision-making elite (Rothchild and Curry 1978: 146). Such an assumption is questionable, yet it underpins a second major link between modernisation theory and the more recent public policy approaches. This is the important role that the focus on order and elites occupies in both modes of analysis. To place great stress on the fundamental role of decision-making elites is a way of focusing on, and advocating, order at both the lower level of the nation and at the higher level of the relationship between national elites in the international arena. In this context, Rothchild and Curry share a common assumption with another recently published work, Robert Rothstein's *The Weak in the World of the Strong: Developing Countries and the International System* (1977).

Rothstein's book is clearly devoted to a different aspect of the problems of Third World countries from Curry's. But the two works share a common methodology: both are concerned with discussing and analysing decision-making and public policy in the Third World and both are committed to the importance of order and the role of elites in the public policy process. Thus, both are typical of much of the recent policy literature on the Third World. Rothstein is concerned with how Third World decision-makers can get the best of a bad deal from the existing international economic order without altering fundamentally the environment within which the dealing takes place. The essence of the book is its stress on improving the Third World's ability to conduct deals, or improving its bargaining position, primarily on an individual state basis as opposed to a collective basis. Such problems are approached through improving the decision-making and policy-implementing capabilities of Third World elites. Rothstein argues that only if elites are maintained in a relatively secure position, with a reasonably long-term perspective, will they indulge in programmes that have long-term benefits (Rothstein 1977: 33). The corollary of this emphasis on elite stability in the recent public policy of development literature is a focus on the need for highly centralised forms of government. In this context, the work of Huntington on the level of institutionalisation in new states has been particularly influential in the 1970s. Huntington believes that the degree of government, not its form, is the key distinction in deciding whether or not policy will be implemented (Huntington 1968: 1-2). This distinction has been used by policy analysts in the 1970s — for example, Joel Migdal (1977).

Implicit in Migdal's approach to public policy in the Third World is the need to concentrate power. The study of public policy is in fact taken over by what one observer has referred to as 'the illusion of bureaucratic and technocratic omnipotence' (Lehmann 1974: 18). Such an illusion is, of course, not uncommon in development studies. Yet the advocacy of bureaucratic centralisation in Third World policy-oriented literature would appear to prevail, despite the acknowledged problems that beset industrial societies in the face of growing centralisation. Further, there is a growing recognition that similar problems of bureaucratisation face many Third World countries, as witnessed in Africa by Ruth First (1971: 105-11), Issa Shivji (1976: 63-99) and other researchers.

Migdal outlines a series of policy failures in the Third World, in places as far apart as Guatemala and Thailand, which he argues are due to 'failures in efforts at political centralisation' (Migdal 1977: 245).

For government intervention in the economy and the polity to be successful greater centralisation is needed; but greater centralisation is prevented, Migdal would argue, by three factors: competing *national* elites which inhibit the capabilities of the national decision-making elites; competing *local* elites, whom the national decision-making elite cannot successfully incorporate into their area of jurisdiction; a passive resistance emanating from aspects of traditionalism 'which siphon off the participation and commitment of the mass of the population from the state's own institutions' (Midgal 1977: 245). It is this resistance to governmental action at the local level, be it positive opposition from elites or mass passivity, which makes the successful implementation of policy extremely difficult.

It is not my intention to argue that Midgal is fundamentally wrong in his analysis, indeed there is much validity to what he says. There are, however, two important points that need to be made. First, Midgal, as a contemporary policy analyst, does in fact exhibit modernisation theory's negative view of tradition. Writing in 1977, he managed to ignore all that was written over the previous ten years concerning the inadequacy of the tradition—modernity dichotomy. Any improvement in the policy-making environment he represents as based upon the breaking down of traditional cultural and social institutions which are seen as barriers. There is also an ethnocentrism in a view which sees improvement in the policy-making process as greater centralisation, bureaucratisation and technological control. Issue has to be taken with the all-embracing nature of a view which does not recognise the importance of such factors as the nature of a *specific* policy or that opposition to policy *might* be rationally based as opposed to stemming from a blind support of tradition.

To the extent that the literature on public policy in the Third World is concerned with the ability of the centre to exercise political and administrative power and authority over the periphery, in arbitrary fashion if necessary, it differs little from the order-based modernisation theory of the later 1960s. The difference between the literature of the early 1960s and that of the 1970s is that, in the former, modernisation theorists tend to assume the presence of centralised power while the writers of the 1970s, drawing on the work of Huntington and Binder *et al.*, make no such assumption.

Given the growing emphasis on order and centralisation in the late 1960s and early 1970s, it is hardly surprising that there is also an emphasis on decision-making and policy-making approaches, as opposed to a focus on long-term planning. In fact, Rothstein points out how an emphasis on survival distorts elite choices towards short-run projects aimed at regime maintenance (1977: 184). But the evidence that secure elites have a more successful record than insecure elites in supporting long-term economic and social development policies is at best ambiguous, as Rothstein is prepared to acknowledge (1977: 197).

That there is a tendency towards elite maintenance as a priority, despite the fact that ambiguity surrounds their recent history, is testimony to the pessimism that engulfed political development theory in the 1970s. In Africa, for example, there has been a clear de-radicalisation of second-generation elites as, on the basis of the experiences of their predecessors, they recognise the magnitude of development problems. Today's African elites do not have the symbolic or the psychic tools at their disposal that their predecessors could mobilise in the euphoric and optimistic period of decolonisation. Second-generation elites thus tend to operate in a different manner from first-generation elites. Similarly, if we contrast theory with practice, then the period of the early 1960s was characterised by political development theory's obsession with mobilisation systems and charismatic authority. In contrast, the 1970s were characterised by the gloomier, more conservative, and evidently more realistic prognosis that emphasised machine politics and authority based on a spoils system and patrimonialism.[6] Henry Bienen (1971) has argued that we are, in fact, seeing the 'Latin Americanization' of Africa in which elites cooperate against the rest of the population in a form of spoils system (which operates with limited resources).

While recognising that not all Third World elites are totally cynical about the future of their countries, Rothstein, like the earlier modernisation theorists such as Weiner, Pool and Huntington, argues that passivity and moderate or low rates of social and economic progress are necessary prerequisites for order and elite maintenance. A sense of futility among Third World elites prompts them to 'take the money and run — or . . . take the money and hide behind the army or the police' (Rothstein 1977: 199). Rothstein argues that it is therefore necessary to devise policy-making systems for Third World states that do not threaten the security of existing regimes nor promise only long-term benefits. Such an emphasis has the effect of institutionalising the major indicator of elite or sub-elite status in Third World states: that is, a privileged position for the group that has been referred to, among other things, as a 'pseudo bourgeoisie' (Amin 1973: 63), 'intendant class' (Cohen 1972: 249) or more generally 'comprador bourgeoisie' (Ake 1976: 7). Basically, this group is supposed to occupy the major decision-making roles in the community on behalf of their own and external interests.

If we see policy analysis as the study of the way in which these groups try to make the best of an existing situation at both national and international levels,then, in light of their dominance of the state and para-state structures, the emphasis on how change in the role of these groups within a given society might be brought about is only a secondary consideration. By focusing on decisions and decision-making, policy-oriented literature fails to tackle a problem considered to be fundamental in most current discussion of politics in new states. This is the role of the post-colonial state. Policy approaches effectively operate at and below the level of the state rather than including the state within a wider analytic framework. Chapter 4 of this work will provide discussion of a form of analysis which will suggest that such inadequacies can and must be rectified.

In most Third World states, politico-administrative power is the chief avenue of access to economic power and personal wealth. In many ways, therefore, policy analysis can act as a vehicle for helping ruling elites improve their position. This is especially true in relation to the external environment. Few would doubt that the policy process in new states is penetrated by external interests, be they former colonial relationships or more recently acquired transnational economic relationships. In such a situation the aim of most elites seems to be to improve their standing *vis-à-vis* these intrusive elements and not to overthrow the existing structure within which the relationship exists. The recent demands for a New International Economic Order must be seen in this context. By blaming most of the ills of their countries on the inegalitarian structure of international economic relations that exist outside national boundaries, Third World elites are able to shed part of their responsibility for many of the problems that exist within national boundaries. While policy analysis cannot be 'blamed' for such a situation, it does, nevertheless, support Third World elites by focusing on the rules of the games at the expense of the nature of the game itself.

Discussion of the strengths and weaknesses of dependency theory, or structural dependence models, follows in the next chapter. Suffice it here to assert that, to date, policy approaches in the Third World have taken little cognisance of this literature. In part, the neglect by policy analysts of the Third World's structurally dependent position can be attributed to Western intellectual origins. Because policy analysis was initially developed for use in Western countries, especially North America, it was not necessary to take account of exogenous factors. The impact of a colonial heritage, foreign aid (in the form of money or personnel) and the overwhelming influence of multinational involvement are factors that are largely unique to Third World states. Policy-oriented literature has assigned a low priority to the way in which the decision-making process in many Third World nations is still dominated by the continued cultural hegemony of the former colonial power. Yet the diffusion of an 'international political culture', brought about by the transfer of Western ideas, values and institutions, as Almond and others predicted in the early 1960s, has occurred. Third World elites do seem to have imbibed many aspects of Western political culture. This is 'primarily a culture of organisations dominated by bureaucratic and technical specialists who place a predominant value on order, pre-dictability and rational calculation' (Berman 1974: 10). However, while it was initially believed that this process of cultural diffusion would be a large-scale exercise that would gradually encompass the populations of Third World states, with the pessimism of the 1960s and the focus on 'order' that replaced democracy as the dominant value, the goal became more limited. The creation of dominant elites became suffic-ient. It is in this context that the emphasis on elite maintenance in recent literature on public policy can be seen as a direct inheritance from modernisation theory.

The Public Policy of Development: a Methodological Critique

In Chapter 4 some of the general problems of the public policy approach as it stands in relationship to the other major school of thought will be discussed. It is perhaps appropriate to conclude this chapter, however, by raising some of the more specific methodological questions prior to the more broad-ranging discussion which is to follow in Chapter 4. The first specific problem that requires discussion is, in fact, a perennial one in the study of the Third World: the problem of the transfer of methods of analysis devised in a 'Western industrial' situation to a non-industrial environment. Such problems beset political science during the 1950s and 1960s, and there seems to be no reason why these problems should mysteriously disappear in the 1970s and 1980s. It is not my intention to argue that it is impossible to transfer policy-making methodologies to the Third World. Rather, in view of the failures of the 1960s, it is instead suggested that much caution is needed as application proceeds — as it surely will given the proven desire of Third World elites to attempt to 'import solutions' from the advanced industrial West (Hirschman 1975: 395).

Several factors that limit the prospects of transferability need to be noted. First, policy analysis's intellectual roots in Easton's systems-process models would not seem well suited to a Third World chiefly characterised by feebleness of governmental institutions and structures. In the West, there has been a tendency to emphasise inputs (political parties, pressure groups, articulation and aggregation functions) at the expense of outputs. Yet, in the Third World a situation predominates in which interests are only infrequently articulated or aggregated and policy inputs are often impossible to identify clearly (Smith 1973: 245).

A second important issue that might limit the successful application of a policy-oriented approach in non-industrial societies stems from the approach's broader, though not exclusive, origins in the pluralist tradition of political science. Central to these traditions is a belief that policy is made by a process of political bargaining and that it represents adjustments between competing group demands and pressures. The consequence of such a view is that policy cannot always be anticipated or radically changed, but merely modified. In policy analysis, such a view came to be conceptualised as 'incrementalism' (Lindblom 1959). Incrementalism is not necessarily central to all strands of policy analysis. Dror (1968), for example, developed a model for policy analysis that has had significant impact on recent administrative theory but which does not have incrementalism as one of its central tenets.[7] But the emphasis on incrementalism needs to be seen as a reflection of its role in the literature on policy-making in the Third World.

Incrementalism has normally been conceived as incompatible with planning, while planning has long been deemed central to efforts to tackle the problems of development − in theory if not in practice. This was especially evident during the first UN Development Decade; every Third World government had to have its 'development plan', even if its purpose was primarily cosmetic and political. This obsession with planning characterised the early periods of development studies when a belief in the efficacy of planning was dominated by 'grand theory' and the expectation of rapid and large-scale social and economic change. It was believed that planning had to be comprehensive while incrementalism, because it rested on the bargaining between and reconciliation of group interests, could never have anything but a problematic commitment to the future.

Things have changed considerably over the last decade. Today, the tendency is to argue that planning and incrementalism are *not* incompatible in Third World policy. Rothchild, Curry and Rothstein all adopt a favourable stance towards incrementalism. While such a position would have been very unlikely in the 1960s, it is entirely in keeping with the pessimism and 'sense of realism' that pervades most of the literature on development in the 1970s. A commitment to planning still exists, of course, but it is much more limited in its scope and expectations than during the 1960s. Rothstein, for example, recognises that planning is not a purely technical phenomenon, but that it is in fact part of, and limited by, the political process; thus it must be related to issues of elite and regime maintenance (Rothstein 1977: 210-12). Short-term decision-making might be incorporated into a broader long-term form of 'indicative' planning — 'a nondirective but influential effort to set general guidelines' (Rothstein 1977: 211). But the utility of incrementalism in the Third World is somewhat ambiguous, and several issues are in need of consideration.

Problems of cultural relativity are at the forefront of any discussion, especially with respect to the pluralist origins outlined earlier. Pluralism in general and incrementalism in particular have been under serious attack in North America over the last decade. Contrary to the earlier beliefs about the value of limited conflict that operates in a consensual framework and offers protection for various groups in the community, there has been a realisation that minorities have not been adequately or properly represented. To what extent is the political theory of pluralism, which is the basis of incrementalism, appropriate as an analytic tool for studying industrial countries, let alone Third World states? The major criticism of pluralism over the last decade is that its emphasis on observable political behaviour and key issues that generate conflict of interest takes no account of what Bachrach and Baratz (1970) have called the 'mobilization of bias' and 'non-decisions'. If, as they persuasively argue, policy-making in industrial society can only be understood by consideration of 'non-decisions' as well as 'decisions', then a similar constraint must surely have equal, if not greater, validity in the Third World.

I would contend that the 'mobilization of bias' and 'non-decisions' are as readily observable in the study of international relationships between Third World states and various organisations as they are, for example, in Crenson's study of the politics of air pollution in American cities (1971), or in the Bachrach and Baratz (1970) study of race and poverty in Baltimore. The mobilisation of bias through organisational influences is particularly well illustrated in Teresa Hayter's (1971) study of the processes of leverage used by the IMF and other international agencies in their dealings with Third World states. Ruling elites in Third World states are normally loath to act in a manner calculated to alienate their international paymasters, be they international organisations or former colonial powers. Thus it is necessary to incorporate factors that constitute the rationale for inertia and inactivity into the policy sciences.

It is not acceptable for students of the public policy of development to ignore critiques that have developed in the mainstream of the discipline. Yet, unlike the work of Crenson or Bachrach and Baratz in the US, the current literature has proved more or less incapable of raising the status of the 'non-decision' from that of a critical idea to a concept that is manageable and applicable to policy studies in the Third World. The importance of doing this is that it would force the policy analyst looking at Third World states not to take the existing order, be it national or international, as given. A public policy approach to development would then be as concerned with changing the existing environment as it would be with enabling decision-making elites to get the best deal under existing circumstances. Policy differences and policy-making in the Third World have to be examined in the context of their dependence on exogenous factors.

If public policy analysis in the Third World is not broadened beyond the activity of government, conceived as regime maintenance and centralisation, then, as in other areas of public policy, it is in danger of being merely 'instrumental and technocratic' (Lowi 1970: 318-19). The basic point of these criticisms is that if the underlying consensus of values and access to the decision-making arena cannot be taken for granted any longer in North American contexts, then it is certainly futile to expect such assumptions to prevail in the Third World context where the prospect of national values and a national consensus are even more problematic. There is very little agreement on the rules of the political game in most Third World countries, where politics is seen by competing groups in zero-sum terms. Resources, in the broadest sense, are strictly limited and are in no way capable of satisfying all competing demands on the economy and polity. Political activity in the Third World, as Rothstein, Rothchild and Curry point out, is dominated by elite decision-making groups. It seems odd, therefore, to suggest, as Rothstein and others (for example Milne 1972a) do, that an incremental model of policy-making based on the resolution of competing group interests should have a great degree of utility in the Third World context. Is incrementalism a realistic proposition for elite-dominated societies, given its pluralist origins? This would seem to be a particularly important question when one considers that the growth of pluralism in political science was in many ways a counter-development to elite-based theories of power.

In support of incrementalism, Rothstein points to its advocacy of a gradual and evolutionary process of change and its utility as a 'good coping strategy' (1977: 215-21). Because of its low levels of expectation, such a strategy can forestall the kind of rising expectations that predominated in the early 1960s. Put another way, incrementalism encourages the 'return to passivity' advocated by Pool and other order theorists in the 1960s.

Incrementalism might well have utility in some states, depending on prevailing social, economic, regional or ethnic conditions. In some states, elites may welcome it — for example, where the ruling elite, even a small elite, is strongly divided on some specific issue or in states with a high degree of elite heterogeneity and a history of conflict, bitterness and hostility to overcome. Here gradualist approaches would be essential. Nigeria, under a civilian regime in the 1980s, may well prove to be an interesting case to observe. Incrementalism will of course prove difficult for ruling elites to sell, especially in those states in which a radical ideology makes *de rigueur* 'a commitment — at least on a rhetorical if not on a practical level — to rapid social and economic change. For example, incrementalism and notions of 'muddling through' run counter to many of the variants of African socialism as an 'ideology of development'.

What, therefore, makes limited policy analysis and incremental decision-making approaches increasingly popular to contemporary political scientists looking at Third World states? In addition to the reasons of intellectual continuity and change in the political science discipline already outlined, it seems that there is another reason worth discussing. This relates primarily to the changing attitude towards the normative questions surrounding development. Such questions cannot be placed in the background, as was the tendency in the 1960s. At both the international and the national levels the world is fundamentally divided over values pertaining to development. In a perfect world, problems of underdevelopment should be solved, as Apter (1971: 11) has pointed out, 'by increased output'. But we now know that resource output, in its broadest sense, has not been as easy to increase as was naively envisaged at the beginning of the first Development Decade. As such, 'choosing' and 'decision-making' become political questions not of the absolute either/or variety, but of the relative more or less variety (Rothstein 1977: 32-3). Consequently, the search for agreement about norms and values in the Third World becomes very important. Human betterment must be central to policy analysis or the whole purpose of its work is negated.

Such concepts as 'human betterment', 'man's fulfilment' etc., however, raise some very difficult questions. Thus, while the importance of normative issues has been recognised, it is accompanied by the belief that such issues cannot easily be resolved. Such a dilemma probably accounts for one of the major changes in the way development was studied in the 1960s and 1970s, and why policy analysis has grown in importance. During the 1960s, modernisation theory emphasised development as a set of ends of achievements, while in the 1970s, the end product is no longer stressed. Instead, development is now seen as a series of processes.

There is consequently a growing tendency to distinguish between higher-order values, which take on a semi-mystical, religious character, and lower-order goals, which are deemed to be, in some measure at least, attainable. Writing in 1965, David Apter made the distinction between what he saw as 'consummatory' values, or those of meaning, and 'instrumental' values, or lower-order values with a more concrete manifestation. With the more practical orientation of policy analysts in the late 1970s, the distinction persisted in, for example, Rothstein's characterisation of incrementalism encompassed within a broader, less clearly defined, system of indicative planning. Even at the different levels at which the two conceptualisations operate, they are in an unstable, dialectical relationship. Analysts accept the possibility that a lower-order goal, like elite security, may have to be pursued at the expense of a higher-order value such as greater equity. Such preferences are clearly in keeping with the prevailing mood of pessimism. The solutions to contemporary problems of underdevelopment are in many ways simply too fundamental to contemplate. We are today in a period in which reform of any magnitude in the Third World seems problematic; consequently, current research emphasises generalised modes of analysis (though they are more specific than the modernisation theory of the 1960s). Having passed over the difficult questions relating to higher-order values in preference to lower-order goals, the emphasis of recent political science literature on the Third World has tended to be on questions of public policy and policy-making.

Although it is more specific and policy-oriented than modernisation theory, the work of the policy analyst tends toward generalisation. It stresses the nature of the policy-making process at the expense of understanding the specific characteristics of policy-making which might emanate from detailed study of Latin American, Asian or African history and culture. Considerable continuity exists between the methodology of recent policy-analysis work and previous modernisation theory; there is still a tendency to provide theories or models in analysing historical and cultural factors, as opposed to using the data available with which to build models. Policy analysis of the Third World in the 1970s was more problem-oriented than the modernisation theory of the 1960s, but only to the extent that the general public-policy approach in political science is more problem-oriented than was the political science of the behavioural period. We still generalise more about the Third World, on which we have unreliable data, than we do about politics in industrial societies for which the data are far superior.

Concluding Remarks

Implicit, but not articulated, in this chapter has been the suggestion that the major weaknesses of the new public policy approach − apart from some quite significant internal methodological inadequacies − is the essentially limited nature of its concerns. Particularly acute, during its formative years of the mid-1970s, was the lack of attention it paid to questions of international relationships between the haves and have-nots of world society and the role of the state and the nature of class formation in the Third World. These issues are, however, treated in the next chapter, and the question of the synthesis of the competing approaches is dealt with in both Chapter 4 and in the Conclusion. By way of conclusion to the chapter I would instead like to offer some tentative explanation as to why this neglect of crucial issues occurred in the nascent public policy of development throughout the 1970s.

I would refer the reader to the suggested analytical approach held up for consideration in Chapter 1 − particularly (following the work of David Ricci 1977) to the utility of the sociology of knowledge and historiographical analysis, as a way of understanding theory development in the social sciences. Following from such a form of analysis we can see that the political science of political development has not exchanged the tenets of modernisation theory for those of that radical genre of development theory, or more specifically underdevelopment theory, that gained in popularity during the early 1970s. The political science of political development has not undergone the kind of transference of allegiance, or conversion, outlined by Kuhn (1962: 151) as appropriate to a paradigm shift. While radical theory has had a period of rejuvenation during the 1970s it has not, to date, moved from the margins of the academic establishment. Ricci alluded to the importance of a 'professional image' (1977: 23-5) for academicians. It is my contention that the creation and preservation of a professional image in political development studies (a 'Cinderella' branch of political science) has entailed the adoption of the predominant trends within the mainstream of the political science discipline. As such this has meant the adoption of the methodological and substantive tendencies of the post-behavioural era in political science rather than any of the 'alternative' radical forms of analysis to receive scrutiny in the next chapter.

While Chapter 1 held back from asserting the possibility of seeing schools of development theory as tightly paradigmatic, it was suggested that there is, nevertheless, a solidarity amongst (social) scientists which causes them to work within a research programme, broadly defined, and despite the often partial and subjective nature of that programme. Acceptance of such a sociological form of analysis as opposed to a more Popperian brand of positivism makes it thus more sensible to treat the development of the political science of political development as contemporary history as opposed to objective science. Indeed, Ricci cites as a prime example of this process in political science generally the work of the developmentalists of the Social Science Research Council Committee on Comparative Politics (Ricci 1977: 29). Unable to overcome cultural and/or professional biases, they inevitably regard their own work highly, as they treat lightly that of those not confined within the parameters of the research programme. This work, as Ricci points out, was not scientific in the Popperian sense, but ideological in the Kuhnian sense. It was based on the social and cultural orthodoxy of American liberalism. As elaborated by Robert Packenham, its four basic tenets are: (1) change and development are easy; (2) all good things go together; (3) radicalism and revolution are bad; and (4) distributing power is more important than accumulating power. As indicated earlier, such assumptions reflected the optimism of the early phases of the political science of political development.

To a large extent, things remain similar at the beginning of the 1980s to the way they were at the beginning of the 1960s. The political science of political development needs to be seen as sociological orthodoxy, not a sub-discipline of political science initiating empirically testable propositions. Further, it is still highly dismissive of most work operating outside of the paradigm of the discipline. There has, however, been one major change and this is in the assumptions upon which recent research is based. In keeping with the prevailing mood of pessimism which has accompanied the changing political reality of the Third World, the evidence provided in this chapter would suggest that we need to modify the four assumptions Packenham outlined as central to the political science of political development. I would like to suggest that the contemporary political science of political development (the public policy of development) is supported by the assumptions that: change and development are no longer easy; all good things might have gone together in Western development but things are almost the reverse in the contemporary Third World; radicalism and revolution are still bad; consequently, accumulating power (to preserve order, seen in the normative sense as the absence of conflict) becomes more important than distributing power.

The acceptance of such assumptions limits the kinds of question that can be asked about the nature of underdevelopment. In particular, the first, third and fourth assumptions encourage limited problem-solving options such as the recent World Bank-initiated 'poverty oriented' approaches to development. They also encourage elite stability and regime maintenance, irrespective of the nature of the regime, while at the same time discouraging a more fundamental questioning of existing structural relationships.

3 BEYOND THE SOCIOLOGY OF UNDERDEVELOPMENT: DEPENDENCY, MARXISM AND THE STATE

It was argued in Chapter 2 that modernisation theory, or, more specifically, the political science of political development, has undergone an intellectual metamorphosis largely in isolation from 'radical' development theory. It cannot be argued in this chapter that the development of radical theory in the last two decades represents a similarly isolated transformation since the main strands of its intellectual heritage are infinitely more diverse than those of the modernisation school. The 'radical school' has to be seen as an eclectic combination of intellectual thought borrowing from the academic social science of Alvin Gouldner (1970), or orthodox development theory on the one hand, and Marxism (and its derivatives) on the other hand. It is for this reason that I prefer the generic term 'radical' to earlier categories such as 'neo-Marxist' (see Foster-Carter 1973). Much of the radical school is not Marxist and would resist such nomenclature, despite borrowing much of the terminology. As will be seen, the radical school is not bound by a single doctrine and reflects a diversity of approach marked as much by conflict over basic theoretical issues as by consensus.

Following from discussion in the introductory chapters we perhaps need to assert at the outset the strengths and weaknesses of attempting to see radical development theory as a research programme. At its broadest there is certainly a substantial body of literature operating from a different intellectual base to modernisation theory. With the younger generation of students of development studies the influence of behavioural social science has clearly waned at the expense of an eclectic radical theory which as a lowest common denominator accepts 'the interconnectedness of development and underdevelopment, of traditional and modern, and indeed of everything in general' (Foster-Carter 1976: 174).

We can also point to the different terminology that is employed in the radical school. This language, referred to by Peter Berger as 'clue concepts' (Berger 1976: 27ff), is in fact a useful way of distinguishing between our two schools. Indeed, the change in terminology between this and the previous chapter is striking. Surplus, class, dependency, imperialism and modes of production take over from modernisation, nation-building, integration system, function, process, etc. as primary concepts.

Such shared terminology and an acceptance of a dialectical relationship between development and underdevelopment is not, however, a sufficient basis for according paradigmatic status to radical theory. Writing in 1978, Kuhn offers us a relevant modification to his original views on scientific change. A paradigm, he tells us, should not be used to refer to a whole set of elements shared by a school of thought and providing relatively uncritical agreement within the school. Rather it is a much more specific 'disciplinary matrix' made up of models and exemplars (Kuhn 1978: 298). Even at a general level, radical theory is not such a bird; nor is it, to take it to its extreme, 'Frankian Normal Science' exhibiting certain 'puzzles', as Foster-Carter claimed it to be in the mid-1970s (1976: 175). It is, however, legitimate to see it as a more general research programme.

Radical theory exhibits highly pluralistic tendencies (as even Foster-Carter 1978 later acknowledged), taking account of its assumption – not shared by conventional theory – that the problems of underdevelopment are part and parcel of the integrated nature of world capitalism. Indeed Foster-Carter's intellectual development, as seen through his writings of the 1970s and given his assumed status as a biographer/codifier of a neo-Marxist paradigm, testifies to the diversity within the school (see Foster-Carter 1974, 1976, 1978 and especially 1980). While we need therefore to recognise the dangers inherent in 'creating' a school of thought, as Taylor in fact warns us (1974: 17), simply because texts share common problems and operationalise similar terminology, there are, nevertheless, clear heuristic benefits to be gained from some kind of classification, especially if our expressed aim is not to establish the homogeneity of a school but rather to present a historiographical review of theory development highlighting the differences as well as the similarities between existing theories. This was the methodology adopted in Chapter 2 and it will be the methodology adopted in this chapter. There is, however, one difference. While both chapters have a strong chronological emphasis, thematic differences are probably of greater significance in Chapter 3 than they were in Chapter 2.

Using Foster-Carter's initial classification (1974: 69), a distinction should first be made between activists and theorists. This chapter is concerned with the work, for example, of André Gunder-Frank, Paul Baran, Arghiri Emmanuel, Bill Warren, Samir Amin, Immanuel Wallerstein, Geoffrey Kay and Colin Leys (no matter how diverse their views), rather than with the work of political activists-cum-theorists such as Franz Fanon, Régis Debray, Che Guevara, Mao tse Tung or Amilcar Cabral. This initial restriction then allows us to differentiate in a second fashion — regarding points of substantive theoretical disagreement between the various scholars and how the debates surrounding these disagreements have worked themselves out over the last couple of decades. Consequently, using a process of chronological and theoretical reconstruction, this chapter examines three major areas of recent thought:

(1) the historical evolution of dependency theory from its radical structuralist origins and the rekindling of an interest in older theories of imperialism;

(2) the debate that has sprung up as a reaction to the increasingly populist appeal of the 'development of underdevelopment' conceptualisation of André Gunder Frank and his supporters;

(3) the development in the late 1970s of the debate over the nature of class formation and the role of the state in post-colonial society, which has emanated from the perceived weaknesses of the dependency debate.

The discussion that follows introduces a variety of concepts in *sequential* fashion. It is not the intention to suggest that these concepts were not 'known' prior to their introduction, but rather that their introduction into the discussion is a chronological representation of their importance to the development debate at a particular point in time. For example, it is not until the end of the chapter that consideration is given to the role of class formation and the post-colonial state. This is not an oversight, but a reflection of the way the debate was to develop throughout the 1970s.

The Early Intellectual Development of Radical Development Theory

As is now well known, the impetus for the development of dependency theory evolved out of the growing dissatisfaction with the role of the Economic Commission for Latin America (ECLA) and particularly with its failure, during the first UN Development Decade, to comprehend the growing problems of the 1960s. In 1963, Ráoul Prebisch outlined the essentials of what was to be known as a 'structuralist' position in economic development (Prebisch 1963; Love 1980). Although the elements of his position had been outlined as early as 1950 (Prebisch 1950), or some would argue even as early as 1945 in the work of Albert O. Hirschmann (1945 and 1978), it was not, however, until the work of André Gunder Frank began to appear in the mid-1960s that the structuralist position began to gain popular acceptance. It was Frank who initially articulated the view that the development studies of the 1950s and 1960s had been little more than an elaborate apology for neo-colonialism − particularly in their assertions that underdevelopment was an *original* condition pre-dating capitalism and for which capitalism, therefore, could not be held responsible. Along with Paul Baran, whose *Political Economy of Growth* was also not to become influential until the mid-1960s, despite being published in 1957, Frank pioneered the view that the inherited productive structures of the Third World 'blocked' capitalist development.

By the late 1960s and early 1970s a whole genre of literature was beginning to challenge the notion that underdevelopment was an original condition. Historical studies such as Frank[8] and Griffin (1969) on Latin America and the late Walter Rodney (1972) and Samir Amin (1972 and 1973) on Africa were attempting to demonstrate how crucial capitalist penetration had been for the underdevelopment of the Third World. This emphasis on history was the great attraction of the structuralist studies of Latin America and offered what many believed to be a methodological and comparative guide for historical work in other areas (see Ehrensaft 1971), especially when compared with modernisation theory. Some have argued, however, that dependency theory, as the orthodoxy of the seventies, has overcompensated with too great a focus on history (Hopkins 1976). Such criticisms notwithstanding, this emphasis, along with much of the 'revolutionary phraseology' (Kay 1975: 103), was a major reason for dependency theory often being termed Marxist or neo-Marxist, even though its initial protagonists were the radical structuralist, but not Marxist, economists of the ECLA such as Prebisch (Oxall *et al*. 1975: 11). A further factor in Frank's importance was his responsibility for extending dependency theory and the structuralist critique of orthodox development economics to the world of the non-economist, but again not without criticism (see, for example, Nove 1974).

Nevertheless, Frank took the structuralist rejection of the diffusionist capabilities of international trade, capital and technology transfer from the developed to the developing world and formulated his own ideas into the 'development of underdevelopment' thesis. Looking at

Latin America Frank and his contemporaries (such as Dos Santos 1973) argued that while it may have been *un*developed before Western pene-tration, it only became *under*developed after incorporation into the international capitalist system. Development and underdevelopment were seen as linked in a causal relationship in which the advanced industrial West was able to develop only because it was underdeveloping the Third World. The basic point about the type of dependence out-lined by such theorists is that it is *dependent* development or under-development, not *interdependent* development that they see. Dependent development is a by-product of the expansion of dominant nations and tied to the needs of the dominant economy as opposed to the needs of the dependent economy. Frank's predominant image was that of the now ubiquitous metropolis—satellite relationship in which the satellite was kept dependent by a sucking out of surplus to the metropole. Such a description is in many ways a caricature of Frank's work, but it is at the heart of much dependency theory.[9]

Without elaborating further at this stage on the early Latin American conceptualisations of dependency theory, we should perhaps conclude this brief introductory discussion by pointing out that by the end of the 1960s Frank and like-minded scholars had spelt out the fallacy of international dualism − the notion that development and under-development were not interlinked − that had predominated in the orthodox development theory up until that time. Frank and his con-temporaries also brought us back to an approach emphasising the importance of political economy which, despite Nove's admonition that it was poor political economy, could only be an improvement on the strict disciplinary approaches that had operated under the broad rubric of modernisation theory throughout the 1960s.

Discussion so far has been restricted to the growth of dependency theory, but the radical debate in the 1960s is also characterised by a second major input turning on the issue of whether Marx recognised the nature of the 'development of underdevelopment' or not. Foster-Carter (1973) and Avineri (1969) would, for example, argue that Marx saw 'backward' societies (his term) not as *under*developed but simply *un*developed. More recently, however, there has been a challenge to the commonly held assertion that Marx had little or no conception of some kind of 'development-of-underdevelopment' hypothesis, given that he saw a largely inevitable and beneficial role for British capitalism in India. It has recently been argued that this view is simplistic and that we must distinguish two phases in Marx's work: the 1840s-1850s and the 1860s − particularly his writings on India and Ireland in which he 'was very close to perceiving the "development of underdevelopment" in Ireland' (Mohri 1979: 37). Yet Marx didn't articulate a 'development-of-underdevelopment' thesis and those who did, especially Frank, did not rely on Marx's work for their theory-building. Further, Marxists, be they Althusserian like Taylor (1979) or more orthodox like Kay (1975), would be horrified to think of Marx as a 'development-of-underdevelopment' theorist. Where Mohri's work is of utility is not as a 'rescue job' on Marx's attitudes to underdevelopment, but rather as a qualification to some of his more trenchant critics who argued that he had failed to grasp the possibility of an underdeveloping role for British free trade in what was to become the Third World (see, for example, Baran 1957: 140; Kiernan 1974: 198; Sutcliffe 1972: 180-1; Barratt-Brown 1970: xli). What we must note, however is that Marx's work had little influence on the growth of dependency theory in the 1960s — except maybe in a symbolic sense of much of the terminology used. As such, it is more important for us to trace the influence of early twentieth-century writers on imperialism such as Luxemburg (1913), Hilferding (1910), Bukharin (1917), Lenin (1917) and the Liberal Hobson (1902). The tendency has been to attribute great influence to Lenin's work, and lately to acknowledge Hobson's influence on it, but to pay little attention to the other Marxist theorists of imperialism. McFarlane (1978), in a recent corrective to this tendency, highlights the contributions to a theory of imperialism of these various writers.

Much of this work was, however, couched in a Eurocentric mould, as indeed was that of Marx. Lenin, as perhaps the primary example, did not consider the problems of developing countries important. Indeed his dominant theme was the tendency of imperialism to lead to politico-military conflict between capitalist powers as economic competition broke down (see Arrighi 1978: 14-15). Consequently the importance of Lenin to the development of a theory of imperialism is at one and the same time both mythical and real. There is an ambiguity over whether Marxists, when they talk of imperialism, are referring to the whole capitalist system or simply writing about underdevelopment and the international aspects of capitalism (see Owen and Sutcliffe 1972: 312-15). Indeed, lip-service is often paid to Marxist theory in discussions of imperialism where in fact no credit exists. Arrighi (1978: 17, n12) highlights this tendency in the work of Magdoff (1969) and O'Connor (1970). Given this kind of ambiguity and genuflection in the direction of early writers, the important question to ask in this historiography is in what respect dependency theory, the dominant intellectual force of the early 1970s, owes any kind of intellectual debt to early Marxist writing?

Frank's work tended to focus exclusively on the relations *between* advanced capitalist societies and the Third World, whereas early Marxist theories were, of course, much broader. For Lenin the 'colonial question' was only one aspect of imperialism. For Lenin, imperialism was above all capital in search of profit in other capitalist countries rather than capital in search of profits in colonial areas, and this is a major distinction between early writings on imperialism and that post-World War II genre of dependency literature (McFarlane 1978: 2). Similarly, the disagreements between the various theorists of imperialism have borne very little importance for the work of Frank *et al*. Perhaps one significant example can illustrate this point. Lenin saw colonies as a place to invest capital, while Luxemburg, on the other hand, saw them as market outlets for manufactured goods from the mother country.[10] Luxemburg felt that such an effort to establish commodity markets in the colonies would lead to industrialisation and capitalist development, albeit immature and unbalanced, in these areas (Luxemburg 1951: 419). Such a view cannot, of course, be an intellectual underpinning for a Frankian 'development of underdevelopment' theory which perceives colonial penetration as having a predominantly underdeveloping tendency. Indeed it is generally in this context that Marxist theory and dependency theory are in fundamental disagreement. A 'development of underdevelopment' hypothesis is irreconcilably at odds with Marx's dictum: 'The country that is more developed only shows to the less developed the image of its own future.' Despite its inequities capitalism was, for Marx, unquestionably a 'progressive' force. It was, in both a unilinear and teleological sense, an advance on pre-capitalist modes of production. The 'development-of-underdevelopment' hypothesis of Frank, however, stresses exactly the opposite point of view and this is the major theoretical distinction for our purposes.

The increasingly popular and populist dependency literature of the 1960s owed much more intellectually to orthodox development economics, with its emphasis on the international aspects of economic exploitation, than to either Marx or early Marxist writers on imperialism. Indeed, some would argue that it is little more than 'neo-classical refinement' (Hopkins 1976). This brief introduction to early Marxist writings on development has not, however, been an irrelevant digression. As we shall see, Marx, and Marxist writers on imperialism, are really much more important when we come to analyse the responses to and *critiques* of the dependency theory of the 1960s than they are in understanding its initial growth. In fact the flow of influence is in the opposite direction, as dependency theory has in many ways provided a spur for the establishment of an increasingly sophisticated Marxist response. The 1970s saw, if nothing else, an end to the sterility which typified the development debate in the 1960s. This debate is not a contest between sterile ideologies and Frank and his fellow 'dependistas' must be thanked for this. The populist and popular nature of the 'development-of-underdevelopment' hypothesis, especially its identification of capitalism as the cause of underdevelopment, forced orthodox and Marxist development theorists alike to respond to a theory that contradicted the teleological and unilinear assumptions they both shared.

Dependency Theory: the View from the Right

Orthodox and radical critiques of dependency theory do overlap in many of their specific objections. These objections are, nevertheless, formulated from quite different viewpoints and can, therefore, be discussed separately. If we consider orthodox critiques first, our starting point must be their attack on the vagueness and level of generality of the development of underdevelopment hypothesis. While the near universality of Frank's metropolis—satellite dichotomy is one of its major attractions, it is also one of its major weaknesses. In descriptive terms it differs little from modernisation theory's tradition—modernity dichotomy. Consequently dependency theory is as difficult to refute at a macro-level, or apply at a micro-level, as in fact was modernisation theory (see, for example, Hopkins 1975: 16). The orthodox critique goes on to argue the ambiguity of the distinctions between dependency and *inter*dependence, or what is more generally referred to as dependency versus dependence theory. No country, it is contested, is autarchic. Developed, as well as underdeveloped, states have a high reliance on foreign trade, investment and technology etc. Dependency must, therefore, be seen as a sliding scale from rich capitalist states at one end of the scale to poor small underdeveloped states at the other. Dependent growth is not unique to the Third World and must be seen as an essential feature of capitalist growth in general (Lall 1975: 801-8; Nove 1974; Ray 1973).

The effort to establish the superiority of the notion of dependence over that of dependency has led to a strong movement by orthodox theorists to measure dependency in an empirical fashion — specifically with a view to undermining the central notion of the development of underdevelopment hypothesis, that is that capitalism causes underdevelopment. Typical of this work are the recent empirical tests of dependency by Kaufman *et al.* (1975), McGowan (1976), McGowan and Smith (1978) and Smith (1979) and that genre of international political economy operating in a liberal mould which stresses 'transnationalism' in an effort to marry world politics and international economics (see, for example, Bergsten and Krause 1975 and Keohane and Nye 1973 and 1976). This work is an indication that conventional social science had found it necessary by the mid-1970s to take dependency theory seriously, in contrast to the attitude of studious neglect that prevailed in the late 1960s and early 1970s. Some of this empirical work in fact goes a stage further than simply refuting the development of underdevelopment hypothesis. In addition it tries to assert that those states which are more open/receptive to integration into the world economy are the ones that have undergone the quickest rates of economic growth.

Dependence should not, however, be seen as a universal phenomenon of all states with differences that are *quantitative* and not *qualitative*. James Caporaso has drawn for us the important distinction between dependence — 'the external reliance on other actors' and dependency — 'the process of incorporation of the less developed countries into the global capitalist system and the "structural distortions" resulting therefrom' (Caporaso 1978: 1). Dependency is not merely quantitative and reducible to purely empirical analysis, rather it is a syndrome of asymmetry (Duvall 1978). The distinction between dependence and dependencia is not merely an exercise in semantics but rather a misrepresentation that can be largely explained by the need for positivist social science to respond to the challenge thrown up by radical theory over the last decade. It is not my intention to suggest efforts to test dependency theory empirically are irrelevant but rather, following Duvall (1978: 71), that they are not entirely central to a dependency approach. Further, the study of underdevelopment would appear to have been pushed further over the last few years by the radical debate over the appropriateness of dependency theory than by these more conventional limited and technical critiques pertaining to the nature of dependence. Such critiques can be of relevance if they can be incorporated into the broader debate about the nature of dependent capitalist development in the Third World and its implications for class formation and the role of the state. The economic reductionism of empirical testing to date has, however, ignored the less quantifiable aspects of dependency such as the nature of the social structure, class interests and class formations, and the general socio-political legacies of colonialism, in a way that critiques of dependency 'from the left' have not.

Beyond the Sociology of Underdevelopment: the View from the Left

While it is not really adequate to argue, as Foster-Carter (1976) has done, that dependency theory became the new paradigm, its role as an intellectual springboard for radical development theory should not be underestimated. Recent developments in radical theory have to be seen as an attempt to go beyond dependency theory. There would appear to be two related, but nevertheless identifiable, streams in this movement: first, a group of writers who have attempted to modify and refine dependency theory's emphasis on the inequality of exchange relationships between the First and Third World — this group we may call 'circulationists'; second, a group of writers who, in more orthodox Marxist vein, have stressed the importance of historical materialism and modes of production — this group we may call the 'productionists'. Both groups, however, refine their theory on the basis of a series of general criticisms of dependency theory that became popular in the second half of the 1970s. The first of these in fact appeared as early as 1971 when Ernesto Laclau took issue with Frank's perceptions of capitalism. Laclau argued that Frank's definition of capitalism was so broad that virtually nothing was excluded from his categories. Frank's inability to distinguish between different modes of production within the same system caused him to believe that *any* production for a market must mean the existence of a capitalist economic system. The problem with Frank's emphasis on the penetration of the Third World by the capitalist market was that it left little or no room for explaining the coexistence of different modes of production, be they capitalist or non-capitalist, at national, regional and local levels (Laclau 1971; Long 1977: 84-7). As Laclau pointed out, the capitalist *economic system* was not the same as the capitalist *mode of production*.

Further criticisms also developed of dependency theory's apparent circularity in trying to explain what actually causes underdevelopment. It is, for example, difficult to sustain the view that the development of advanced industrial capitalism was *only* possible by the exploitation of the periphery. That the rise of the West may have been *in part* facilitated by such factors as the slave trade and the colonisation of India is not in much dispute, but it is an argument of a different order to suggest these were overriding, as at times do Baran (1957: 144-50), Frank (1969) or Rodney (1972).

The development-of-underdevelopment hypothesis soon came to be recognised as not being universally applicable. Pre-colonial units were not always destroyed by capitalist penetration and indeed in some areas colonial policy effectively capitalised on pre-capitalist structures (see Ehrensaft 1971). Further, dependency theory's emphasis on the impact of colonialism as the main source of change ignored important socio-cultural factors that needed to be recognised as enhancing or hindering exogenously induced change.

Bill Warren (1973), in what was to be acknowledged as a seminal work, further extended the critique of dependency theory's confused view of capitalism. Its weakness, he too argued, lay in its assertion that capitalism *caused* underdevelopment, since such an assertion denied the possibility of development taking place in the Third World *within* a capitalist framework. Using aggregate data, Warren went on to assert that *per capita* growth rates in the Third world have in fact outstripped population growth. Further, contrary to the view of the dependistas, it has not all been 'growth without development'. Economic contact between advanced industrial society and the Third World can promote economic development and has done so. Industrialisation, Warren's yardstick for economic development, has in fact taken place at a much greater rate in some areas than dependency theorists have been prepared to concede. Such a situation, Warren argued from an orthodox Marxist stance which accepted the dialectical process, will bring about capitalism and subsequently generate proletarian revolution. What Warren was effectively saying, in contradiction to early dependency theorists, was that a middle ground of countries is developing between the First and Third worlds — thus undermining a simple centre—periphery conceptualisation.

Warren was of course vigorously criticised, particularly by Emmanuel (1974) and McMichael, Petras and Rhodes (1974). The essence of their critiques related to Warren's selection of data and the dangers of aggregating statistics for countries as diverse as Taiwan and Singapore on the one hand and, say, some of the poorer land-locked states of Africa on the other. This debate is not, however, particularly central to our intellectual history. Notwithstanding the accuracy of these methodological criticisms. Warren's work, along with Laclau's, effectively represented the beginnings of a Marxist alternative to the development-of-underdevelopment hypothesis. Again, notwithstanding criticisms about the inegalitarian nature of the kind of development Warren pointed to, Warren effectively undermined that early pietistic assertion of much dependency literature that formal political independence, namely decolonisation, made little or no difference to the development process in the Third World. Some peripheral states have quite clearly demonstrated a capacity for some sustained growth and a consequent improvement in their structural position in the international economy, no matter how slight (Warren 1973: 20 and also Cardoso 1973).

It is accepted that Third World industrialisation was largely restricted to urban areas, was lop-sided and that it produced an extremely uneven spread of benefits. The basic point is that Warren raised a series of questions about a dependency approach which were to dictate the paths that the radical debate was to take in the second half of the 1970s. This path, largely ignored by dependency theorists operating in a Frankian mould, led to a growing scrutiny of class formation in the Third World and the role played by the post-colonial state in the development process. It also led to a breaking down of the largely un-differentiated 'Third World' conception that had prevailed at the turn of the decade. An acceptance, or rather recognition, of the existence of a group of semi-peripheral states caused us to begin to distinguish between that group of states where some kind of national system of economic power was being built and those states where capitalist penetration and consequent industrialisation had been much less influential.

To review briefly our discussion to this stage. Radical critiques of dependency theory to the mid-1970s revolved around the supposed ability, or otherwise, of capitalism to generate capitalist growth at the periphery. Dependency theorists emphasised economic stagnation at the periphery and the extraction of surplus[11] from the Third World — particularly important were the perceived mechanisms of surplus extraction; trade, aid, finance and investment controls, profit repatriation, debt servicing, etc. Pierre Jalée's *The Pillage of the Third World* (1968) and Harry Magdoff's *The Age of Imperialism* (1969), along with Frank's work, were prime examples of this genre of literature. Marxists, on the other hand, came to express a contradictory point of view. In mounting a challenge to dependency theorists they questioned the reliability of a development of underdevelopment hypothesis which seemed to reject the positive impact of international capital and technology. The essence of this position, outlined by Luxemburg at the turn of the century (McFarlane 1978: 9), has been perfectly captured in Geoffrey Kay's now celebrated statement that:

> The radical critiques of orthodox development theory were so keen to prove the ideological point that underdevelopment was the product of capitalism, that they let the crucial issue pass them by: capital created underdevelopment not because it exploited the underdeveloped world, but because it did not exploit enough (Kay 1975: x but see also Robinson 1976: 46 and Emmanuel 1976: 760).

It is in this context that Luxemburg and other early writers on imperialism were clearly more the intellectual precursors of authors such as Warren, Emmanuel and Kay than they were of Frank and the dependistas. As unpalatable as it might be for some of revolutionary persuasion, it has to be recognised that industrialisation growth rates in the 'Sweat Shops' of South-East Asia have outstripped those in some revolutionary societies (see Petras 1975: 291 and Warren 1973: 16). In recognising, or rather acknowledging, this situation, writers such as Warren *et al.* cut a swathe through the ideology of dependency theory, which had been as keen to recognise the underdeveloping tendency of world capitalism as was modernisation theory to recognise capitalism's developing tendencies. Dependency theory's Latin American origins and its emphasis on the exploitation of 'agromineral societies' (Petras 1975: 292) was only a partial view of the Third World and inappropriate for many other areas, particularly South-East Asia, but also large parts of Africa. The early universalist dependency theory ignored such simple and unfashionable factors as, for example, the geo-politics of land-locked coastal dichotomies in the Third World, initial factor endowments such as climate, natural resources and population and the resulting effect of these factors on the subsequent degree of colonial penetration of a particular area.

There have, however, been significant refinements to these earlier, relatively unsophisticated views of dependency. These refinements have managed to take account of such criticisms without crossing totally from a dependista to a more orthodox Marxist position. The three most significant actors in this context have probably been Arghiri Emmanuel, Immanuel Wallerstein and Samir Amin, whom we might categorise as the most sophisticated of the post-Frankian 'circulationists'.

Circulationists and Productionists

Circulationism

Since it was in many ways a continuation of dependency theory, albeit seasoned by the work of Fernand Braudel from the French 'Annales' school (Hockey-Kaplan 1978: 9), Immanuel Wallerstein's World Systems Theory (WST) did not have the same 'breakthrough effect' as did the work of André Gunder Frank. Wallerstein may certainly have refined some of the more obvious simplicities of the early dependency theory, but WST has to be seen originating from a similar intellectual stable to the extent that it views capitalist development as a global process which produces and reproduces growing inequality within and between the world's states.[12] Further, along with Samir Amin, Wallerstein shares dependency theory's rejection of the previously outlined views of Marxist theorists of imperialism. They do this to the extent that they see a flow of capital from the periphery to the centre by a process of unequal exchange rather than accept a Leninist view of the expansion of imperialism as necessary for the realisation of surplus value in the centre. For Lenin and Luxemburg it was, as has been noted, the inability to realise surplus value at the centre which caused imperial expansion to provide export markets. Wallerstein and Amin can thus be termed 'circulationists' to the extent that they concentrate on exchange relations and, in so doing, are greatly influenced by Arghiri Emmanuel's notion of unequal exchange (Emmanuel 1972). In this context Emmanuel's influence on the radical debate has been of sufficient significance for it to be considered briefly in its own right.

For Emmanuel, and by extension for Amin and Wallerstein, trade serves a contrary function to that viewed by Lenin and Luxemburg. By a process of unequal exchange capital flows to the metropole, capital does not flow out of the metropole to the Third World in search of use. The process of unequal exchange between the centre and the periphery is due to wage differentials. Lower wages at the periphery, Emmanuel argues, allow for the extraction of a higher surplus value which is siphoned to the centre. This is itself a major refinement of the work of early dependency theorists whose notions of a 'sucking out of surplus' were rudimentary in the extreme. Emmanuel's refinement relates to his disagreement with the initial diagnosis of the deterioration of the terms of trade by dependency theorists, as initially outlined by ECLA economists such as Prebisch in the 1960s. As Emmanuel points out:

The worsening of the terms of trade for primary products is an optical illusion. It results from a mistaken identification of the exports of rich countries with the exports of manufactured goods and the exports of poor countries with the exports of primary products (Emmanuel 1972: xxx).

He is not denying that the exports of poor countries are dominated by the export of primary produce, rather he is arguing that the terms of trade deteriorate not against primary products but against poor countries; for Emmanuel, the nature of the commodity is irrelevant. Such a situation results from what he calls 'unequal exchange' in which, as indicated, the difference in wage rates between rich and poor countries is the key factor.

Emmanuel's theory throws up a major challenge to the dominant Ricardian notion that international trade is beneficial to *all* those who participate. This attack on the theory of comparative advantage is supported by both Wallerstein (1978) and Amin (1976: 18). Emmanuel has attracted a good deal of criticism from, what I call somewhat uncomfortably, orthodox Marxist critics.[13] In this he is not, however, alone. Considerable objection has been lodged against Wallerstein's conceptualisation of the 'world capitalist economy' in which all states operate as 'capitalist', even if they are 'socialist' states, within a single world market. Wallerstein argues that there is only a single international division of labour dominated by the only mode of production — global capitalism — but which does comprise sub-parts which are alternative 'modes of labour control'. Within this international division of labour there are regional differences and specialisations linked to the world economy by the operation of the market (Wallerstein 1974: 67-129 and 1964b: 390). To put it another way, for Wallerstein, global capitalism is characterised as commodity production for profit in the world market and this form of production articulates a variety of forms of labour exploitation within the context of asymmetrical relations between powerful states and peripheral areas (1974: 126-7). While Wallerstein prefers the term 'dependent capitalist' to 'underdeveloped' states at the periphery, he is in fact accepting a form of dialectic of development and underdevelopment. Wallerstein does, however, add an important dimension to a core/periphery or metropolis/satellite conceptualisation. He sees a group of semi-peripheral states existing between the core and the periphery. These can be either declining core states or rising peripheral ones (inconsistent with a development of underdevelopment hypothesis?). Further, Wallerstein sees them as stabilising middlemen preventing a polarised world (see Wallerstein 1974a); as both exploiter and exploited they act as a buffer.

Wallerstein's conceptualisation is based on market or exchange relations as opposed to production relations. The intellectual origins of such an approach are clearly not Marxist. Crompton and Gubbay (1977: 5-19) allude to the obvious Weberian links of an approach based on exchange relations, while others have demonstrated in great detail the relationship between Wallerstein's work and that of classical economists such as Adam Smith — particularly the emphasis on a trade-based division of labour (Brenner 1977: 38). In this context, despite its refinements, Wallerstein's approach is as little different and equally unacceptable for orthodox Marxists than it was when Laclau established his productionist critique of Frank in 1971. Indeed Depuy and Fitzgerald (1977) establish a similar critique of Wallerstein. Also, similar to the objection to Frankian dependency theory expressed earlier, Wallerstein has been criticised from both the right (Smith 1979: 252-7) and the left (Trimberger (1979: 128) for his generality; for his desire to 'totalise' the study of society at the expense of historical specificity. Even those who advocate a form of Wallersteinian analysis[14] recognise that a major weakness is the generality of its methodology (Hockey-Kaplan 1978: 15).

The third important 'circulationist' in need of discussion is Samir Amin who, despite writing prior to Wallerstein on these issues, did not come to be recognised as important in the English-speaking world until the translation of his major theoretical works into English in the mid-1970s. Especially important was his *Accumulation on a World Scale* (1974) and *Unequal Development* (1976). Amin has played an important bridging function in several ways. First, in a way that Frank and Wallerstein have been unable to do, he has broken down the highly monolithic manner in which WST perceived the world capitalist system (for an excellent review see Leaver 1979). Second, Amin tends to straddle our competing circulationist and productionist views. This bridging role can be seen in Amin's reliance on the work of Althusser and Poulantzas, especially for his explanations of social class, and in his reliance on the work of French Marxist economic anthropologists such as Rey, Terray, Meillassoux and Coquery-Vidrovitch in his discussion of modes of production (see, for example, Amin 1976: Ch. 1).

At the centre of Amin's work is the notion of 'accumulation on a world scale' — being a transfer of surplus from pre-capitalist to capitalist modes of production which comes about in an Emmanuelesque type of unequal exchange between centre and periphery. Amin's model of global accumulation sees two distinct patterns of development for the centre and the periphery. In the centre, economic development is characterised by the satisfaction of mass consumer needs. At the periphery, economic activity is characterised, on the one hand, by the production of luxury goods (or their importation) for a small elite and, on the other hand, by the production or extraction of primary produce or resources for export (Amin 1974a). To this extent Amin goes along with Frank and Wallerstein in arguing that an understanding of underdevelopment (Frank) or dependent capitalism (Wallerstein) requires an acknowledgement of the dominance of capitalism as a world system with global exchange relations providing a coherent accumulation process. Similarly, he accepts, along with Frank and Wallerstein, some kind of notion of 'blocked development', especially in his early work (see Amin 1973 and 1974). Indeed, his *Neo-colonialism in West Africa* (1973) was originally published in French as *l'Afrique de l'Ouest Bloqúee* (1971).

Amin does, however, part company with Frank and Wallerstein on two very specific issues. First, he rejects the central importance of the 'sucking out of surplus' from the periphery to the centre for development in the centre. Second, he rejects their notion of the existence of merely one mode of production – namely the Capitalist World System. For Amin, the Capitalist World System is a combination of capitalist (in its pure form at the centre) and non-capitalist modes of production (albeit in distorted form) which are combined at the periphery in a variety of social formations. His emphasis on the possible variety of social formations at the periphery is at one and the same time his great strength and his great weakness. It is instructive here to compare the detail Amin provides on the uniqueness of peripheral social formations in *Unequal Development* (1976) with Frank's early rudimentary distinction between metropolis and satellite. This spatial distinction in their work can also be contrasted with a comparable temporal distinction. Amin (1976) and Wallerstein (1976) have been at the forefront of that group of radical scholars who see the need to 'periodise' the stages of capitalism – unlike Frankian analysis which envisaged only feudalism and capitalism. Such a view recognises potential conflicts where the Frankian view tended to emphasise continuities. But even Amin, despite advancing beyond the rigidly structured Frankian view, does not provide a truly adequate classification of the complex array of relationships that might be possible at the periphery. This comment is made without prejudice to Amin's very real attempts to categorise a variety of social formations (see Amin 1976: Ch. 5). It is, of course, to be doubted whether any such classification is possible, since the varying spatial and temporal distinctions provide the possibility for as many combinations as cases. The importance of Amin's work on social formations is that it transcends, or provides a bridge between, the views on the circulationists, with their emphasis on one world capitalist system, and the productionists, with their emphasis on the articulation of various modes of production at the periphery.

Productionism

There is, of course, a good deal of confusion surrounding the notions of mode of production and social formation. Marx himself provided a detailed analysis of the capitalist mode of production, but little or no discussion of non-capitalist modes. This task has been picked up largely by contemporary Marxists in the post-colonial era; especially the French Marxist economic anthropologists such as Terray (1972), Godelier (1977) and Meillassoux (1972),[15] and more recently the English sociologist Taylor (1979).

This work has been strongly influenced by Althusserian structura-. ism, variously and not at all flatteringly described as 'a meta-physical conception of Marxism inhibited by reified structures' (Alavi 1979: 5) or as 'structural functionalism clothed in marxist concepts' (Foster-Carter 1978: 56). The debate over modes of production in the 1970s can, at best, be seen as a plethora of interminable and very often indigestible definitional debates (see Law 1978). Some kind of clarity pertaining to the central issue, namely the distinctions between modes of production and social formations, would, however, appear to be emerging from this structuralist fog; although it should be noted that such clarification would seem to be due largely to the efforts of authors of a non-structuralist persuasion (see, for example, Alavi 1979 and Mouzelis 1980). In a manner seemingly impossible to most Marxist practitioners in the field of underdevelopment, Robert Cox, for example, by returning to Marx's own notions, has provided a most succinct précis of what would appear to be the distinction between a mode of production and a social formation:

> The mode of production was his deductive model that enabled him to explore the properties and dynamics mainly of capitalism and to a more limited extent precapitalist forms, as in *Capital*. The social formation was his framework for analysing the interaction of different forms of production and social classes in a particular historical conjuncture, e.g. France following the revolutions of 1848 in his

Eighteenth Brumaire of Louis Bonaparte (Cox 1979: 290-1).

Hamza Alavi, from a standpoint critical of the Althusserian productionists, also provides a fairly succinct distinction between the two concepts:

> Social formation is a descriptive concept that denotes an actual and specific societal entity, with all its peculiarities, products of past developments, structuration and restructuration, results of accidents and design and all its legacies of the past and potential for the future. As such it refers to a particular, geographically bounded, historically given entity with given resources, and given forms of economic and political organization and cultural features. . . The concept of mode of production, on the other hand, is a concept of quite a different level for it refers not to the particularities but the underlying structural regularities . . . mode of production is thus not a part of a social formation; it is part of its structure (Alavi 1979: 11).

The mode of production, or modes of production in articulation, gives shape to a particular social formation. A mode of production does not, of course, exist of itself in a material form; 'we cannot speak of "boundaries" of a mode of production in the same sense as we may speak of the boundaries of a social formation' (Alavi 1979: 12).

The centrality of the mode of production in Marx's conception of capitalism has to be acknowledged. Consequently the notion of the articulation of capitalist and non-capitalist modes in the study of underdevelopment is a debate of major concern despite the confusion that surrounds it. It is, for example, extremely important to ask exactly how a dominant capitalist mode of production articulates in the periphery with a non-capitalist, basically commodity-oriented, form of labour power? Laclau's critique of Frank established, in opposition to the view originally held by Frank, that capitalist and non-capitalist modes of production could exist side by side and that the penetration of capitalism did not automatically eradicate pre-capitalist forms — but could, and indeed often did, coexist with and reinforce pre-capitalist modes (Laclau 1971).

Yet the importance of Laclau's critique was not recognised immediately on publication. Frankian dependency theory was at that period in the early 1970s too busy becoming the (albeit brief) orthodoxy of the day for initial critiques to be taken seriously. It was to take several years for the weaknesses to be recognised. Like so many theories, just as it was cresting in popularity, dependency theory's fundamental weaknesses, though not at that stage visible, were beginning to form at the base of the wave. Laclau's critique, as forceful as it was — a fact attested to by its continued regular citation in current work critical of dependency theory (see, for example, Alavi 1979; Taylor 1979; Bernstein 1979; Roxborough 1979) — did not gain recognition until the mid-1970s when it was joined by similar objections to the Frankian conception of capitalist penetration of the periphery. This time lag in recognition again attests to the importance of David Ricci's exhortation to examine theory development in historiographical fashion.

As a Marxist response to dependency theory and world-system theory, mode-of-production theory rejected the Wallersteinian notion of one simple global capitalist mode. With its emphasis on the 'articulation' (see Foster-Carter 1978 for a discussion of this concept) of modes of production within specific peripheral or Third World social formations, modes of production theory established a much more complex view of the relationships between development and underdevelopment. But its major strength at a practical level is its major weakness at a theoretical level. Attempts to 'articulate' modes of production theory without an overall framework within which to operate have seen a profusion and confusion of modes[16] which represents an over-reaction to the macro-analytical framework of world systems theory or the earlier dependency theory. Mode of production theory has little or nothing to say about the structural effects of imperialism, unlike dependency theory in which the structural effects of the global economic system is all. At the risk of over-simplification what we are left with is a 'levels of analysis problem' in which the notion of modes of production in articulation has not proved to be the tool with which radical theorists could link, as they had hoped (see Clammer 1975), the different — local, regional, national and international — levels of analysis. Indeed, the search for a theory of underdevelopment has brought a tone of despair into the work of some authors prominent in the field (see, for example, Bernstein 1979: 91-7 and Foster-Carter 1978: 55).

What has been the outcome of this debate between circulationists and productionists? Despite the weaknesses inherent in both approaches has there been some kind of beneficial synthesis? I'd like to suggest that there has, and that the debate has enabled radical development theory to get over one major stumbling block, at least, which had existed in the first half of the 1970s. Perhaps the major problem of the early and middle 1970s was the enormous ideological appeal of dependency theory's development of underdevelopment hypothesis (in its several forms). Dependency theory undermined, at both a methodological and an ideological level, the assumptions of modernisation theory and highlighted the uneven nature of the development of capitalism on a global scale. Thus the logical solution to the problems of underdevelopment came to be seen as the eradication of capitalism as a world system of unequal exchange relations. The battle lines for the eradication of this system were, therefore, to be between world capitalism as the oppressor and the Third World as the oppressed. Such battle lines pin-pointed the major weakness of dependency theory which I have so far studiously, and with great difficulty, avoided — namely dependency theory's totally deficient understanding of class analysis and its role in the study of underdevelopment. For dependency theory and world systems theory, with their emphasis on unequal exchange relations between a core and a periphery, social classes became synonymous with geographical entities and problems of inequality and deprivation, thus making the prospect of any useful class analysis extremely unlikely. It was only with the appearance of productionist critiques of dependency theory and specific critiques of the banality of dependency theory's class categories (for example Roxborough 1976; Luton 1976; Phillips 1977; Leys 1977; Bernstein 1979) that the debate was able to progress.

The real importance of the productionist debate for contemporary theory undoubtedly lay in its highlighting of the complexity and array of relationships that are possible under global capitalism. The obvious corollary of this is a system of class relationships more complex than that of a dependent Third World bourgeoisie in a comprador relationship with international capital, as epitomised by much of the radical structuralist literature of the first half of the 1970s.

Underdevelopment, Class Formation and the Post-colonial State

Neglect of the issues of class formation and the post-colonial state in the study of underdevelopment has been deliberate. Its purpose was to highlight the artificiality of the dependency debate up to the middle of the 1970s. By the limited nature of its concerns, dependency theory, radical structuralism or whatever, effectively precluded any meaningful discussion of these topics. It was only with the establishment of the productionist critique of the abiding nature of dependency theory's 'development of underdevelopment' hypothesis that the nature of class formation and the role of the state in post-colonial societies could warrant analysis in other than cursory fashion as the inevitable outcome of the prevailing economically deterministic radical structuralism. With the growth of the productionist critique it was no longer satisfactory to assert that the dominant classes of peripheral formations could operate only within a comprador framework. The analysis of class formation at the periphery has become contingent on an understanding of the historical conditions of specific cases of capitalist penetration. In the early part of the 1970s the popular appeal of dependency theory and its subsequent modifications effectively prevented the recognition of such a viewpoint. Several factors subsequently opened the way for the evolution of the debate over class formation and the role of the state in post-colonial societies.

First, Marxist approaches to underdevelopment have been greatly influenced by the changes that have been taking place within the mainstream of Marxist thought. The growing interest in the state and class at the periphery has received considerable impetus from the resurgence of Marxist research on the state in industrial societies that took place in the late 1960s and early 1970s, especially attempts to re-establish the Marxist position over that of the non-class-based analyses of bureaucracy and political power that had characterised the predominant Weberian and pluralist notions of the post-World War II period (Frankel 1978: 17). The subsequent, and celebrated, debates between Miliband and Poulantzas (Poulantzas 1969, Miliband 1970, Laclau 1975) gave a relative sophistication to the Marxist discussion of the capitalist state that had previously been missing. The parallels in the study of underdevelopment would appear obvious. The success of modernisation theory was in part due to the vulgarity of initial Marxist writings on 'backward societies' (for example Baran 1957) and the dormant nature of Marxist theories of imperialism in the wake of the decolonisation process. Vulgar conceptualisations can, of course, be influential, as indeed was the 'development of underdevelopment' in forcing Marxist thinkers to articulate substantive critiques capable of challenging its popular and populist appeal. The outcome of these efforts has been an increasingly sophisticated debate over the nature of class and the role of the state in peripheral societies.

As indicated, the view of class and the state that emanated from dependency theory was one which perceived ruling groups in the Third World — be they industrial/commercial or political/bureaucratic/military and whether knowing or not — as agents of foreign domination.

Working from a simple economic determinism, radical structuralism perceived Third World countries, given their dependence, as incapable of producing an indigenous dominant class capable of serving other than foreign interests. Thus spoke André Gunder Frank in his *Lumpenbourgeoisie: Lumpendevelopment* (1972), the apotheosis of this genre of literature and, albeit in less strident terms, Samir Amin in his *Unequal Development* (1976, first published in French, it needs to be noted, in 1972); or, for example, James Petras, who saw class formation in the post-colonial period as emanating from 'externally directed capital accumulation based on simple surplus extraction' (Petras 1975: 300) and characterised by the development of an intermediary ruling class controlling this process of accumulation on behalf of external interests and through its control of the state apparatus.

The conception of the state that grew out of the predominance of dependency theory in the late 1960s was epitomised in Hamza Alavi's work on the 'overdeveloped' post-colonial state (Alavi 1972). Implicit in this work was a view of the state as a hinge between international capital and Third World social formations. This view of the state was effectively the 'first stage' in the recent debate. This first stage found expression, not only in the work of Alavi and Petras, but also in John Saul's (1974) and Issa Shivji's (1976) work on Tanzania and Colin Leys' early, and extremely influential, work on Kenya (1974). The overdeveloped post-colonial state was, in essence, one which exhibited a certain autonomy (see Miliband 1977: 106ff) from the indigenous class structure *per se*, at the same time as it exhibited control over the production process. In this context the state was seen as a mediator between local and international capital and as a security agent for international capital — what Petras refers to as the state's 'enforcer role' (1975: 302).

Also central to the notion of the 'overdeveloped' post-colonial state was the large military and administrative/bureaucratic apparatus inherited from colonialism and responsible for expropriating and utilising a substantial proportion of the state's economic surplus (see Ake 1976). The consequence of such activity, as Shivji for example would argue, is that the personnel of the state apparatus who take on these functions develop a specific class interest of their own. This group, essentially a class in the making, Shivji referred to as the 'bureaucratic bourgeoisie' (Shivji 1976). He saw them as a class of well paid administrators, military officers and/or party officials appropriating or controlling production with one outcome, at least, being the personal acquisition of private capital. As a class, the bureaucratic bourgeoisie was perceived as having a vested interest in preserving its client role with international capital.

The preceding discussion represents a crude caricature of that conception of class and the state that emerged in the hey-day of dependency theory. Needless to say, the reactions to dependency theory, already outlined, brought forth similar reactions to its accompanying conceptions of class and the state. One of the most vehement critics was in fact Colin Leys, who, in an important auto-critique, acknowledged the influence of such views on his own early work (Leys 1978: 251). Leys, along with others, such as Sklar (1979), has emphasised the narrowness of such a structurally determined view of the role of the state and the nature of class formation. Such views clearly offered little or no prospect of autonomy for the 'political' from the 'economic'. Class politics in the Third World was consequently perceived by dependency theory as 'economically reductionist' (Goulbourne 1979: 17 and Leys 1977: 95). It is in the context of such admonitions that Marxists join, somewhat ironically, with orthodox critics such as Nove and Hopkins in seeing dependency theory, or perhaps more appropriately in this instance the sociology of under-development in general, as being very poor political economy.

From such critiques has sprung an effort, particularly in the work of Colin Leys (1976, 1977, 1978, 1979) in the latter part of the 1970s, to return to a discussion of class and the role of the state anchored in a more secure Marxist intellectual tradition. It should be noted, however, bearing in mind the historiographical aims of this essay, that the basis of such a critique had in fact appeared several years earlier (Warren 1973:39). If we accept the validity of Warren's argument that imperialism does not inevitably prevent the spread of indigenous capitalist development in peripheral formations, in contrast to dependency theory, then we need also to reject a subsequent tenet of dependency theory — namely that increased political independence, in the nominal sense of decolonisation, is irrelevant as a means of facilitating capitalist development (Warren 1973: 10-11). The logical extension to an acceptance of this view is the rejection of a third tenet of dependency theory — in this instance the assertion that the dominant class in any Third World state will, almost by default, be 'comprador' and in a patron-client relationship with international capital. As Richard Sklar has pointed out, such views of class, especially notions of the burgeoning of a bureaucratic bourgeoisie as a functional or structural class, are

> too narrowly conceived to comprehend the dominant class of a developing country that has a significant entrepreneurial sector in

addition to a large and growing number of persons in professional occupations. Theoretically, a functional elite, such as the civil and military bureaucratic elite, by itself could form an elite-class [*sic*]. But this limiting case does not exist anywhere to my knowledge. In all societies, the functionary element is part of a social class, not its sole constituent (Sklar 1979: 544-5).

No researcher, party to this debate conducted largely in the African context, was suggesting — to look at dependency theory's general strengths — that the dominant forces at work in Africa, or the Third World generally, were other than expatriate. What they were not prepared to accept, however, was the restrictive nature of a class analysis based on the notion of the growth of a structurally determined bourgeoisie, be it 'bureaucratic' or whatever. Such a position, as Leys indicated (1976: 48), could only deflect us from asking more important questions about a more numerous and more general dominant class and its relations to the post-colonial state; particular questions about the extent to which the dominant class undermined, as opposed to supported, external interests. As Leys, in his auto-critique of *Underdevelopment in Kenya* (1974), argued:

> Instead of seeing the strength of the historical tendency lying behind the emergence of the African bourgeoisie I tended to see only the relatively small size and technical weakness of African capital in face of international capital, and to envisage the state as little more than a register of this general imbalance; rather than seeing the barriers of capital, scale and technology as the register of the leading edge of indigenous capital in its assault on those barriers (Leys 1978: 251-3).

What Leys and others investigating Kenya (Swainson 1977) were effectively doing was reversing the view of the role of the state that had developed in the first half of the 1970s. The dominant class in Third World states or fractions thereof, it was being argued, could in fact use state power for its own purposes and not just simply for the benefit of international capital. In retrospect such an interpretation appears self-evident, yet to accept such an assumption is not, *ipso facto*, to accept that the way is open for development centred on the economic nationalism of a growing bourgeoisie.

Anne Phillips (1977: 8), for example, warns us that all we may be seeing is the growth in Africa of forms of underdevelopment comparable to those in Latin America. Phillips might have gone on to add that such a process might also be restricted to quite specific areas of Africa. We need to be careful, in our extrapolations from the work of Leys, Swainson *et al.* on Kenya, not to throw out the baby with the bath water. Processes of capital accumulation (and the prospects for capital accumulation) based on factor endowments, the degree of colonial penetration and so on are markedly different in states such as Kenya, Ivory Coast and Zambia than they are, for example, in many of the land-locked states of former Francophone Africa. Consequently, we would do well to bear in mind the variety of stages of development resulting from the variety of combinations of factor endowments and degrees of colonial penetration. Leys himself (1978: 260) points to some of the advantages settler colonialism bestowed on Kenya and Kenya's subsequent position in the East African context which paved the way, relatively speaking in African terms, for significant 'early industrialisation initiatives not to be found in other areas of the continent'. The position of settler capital in Kenya also prevented the degree of penetration of international capital, in relative but not absolute terms, experienced in other states. The subsequent substitution, in the early years after independence, of members of the growing national dominant class at the expense of settlers would appear to have obvious future parallels for a state such as Zimbabwe, given Zimbabwe's favourable factor endowments and very high levels of international penetration.

Very few other African states, however, would appear to exhibit a similar (in Ley's words) ' "systematical combination of moments" conducive to the transition to the capitalist mode of production' (Leys 1978: 261). There are clearly a substantial number of states that possess — in contrast to say Kenya, Zimbabwe, or to a lesser extent Ivory Coast (see Campbell 1978) — extremely small entrepreneurial and professional sectors, exhibiting low or even negative processes of growth and where as a consequence the personnel of the state bourgeoisie constitutes not a fraction but in fact the vast majority of the broad category of people we may call the dominant class. For example, in some of Africa's poorest land-locked states, for the want of any alternative, there is little or no prospect — at this particular conjuncture — for the development of a significant component of the dominant class outside the confines of what we might call a state bourgeoisie (Higgott 1980). Further, it is perhaps more appropriate in such contexts to minimise the role of the state as 'the leading edge of indigenous capital in its assault' on international capital at the expense of a view which sees the state as the 'register of a general imbalance' between domestic and international capital.

It behoves us, therefore, to recognise the variable effect of historical and socio-economic considerations upon different peripheral states. Such a conclusion leaves the debate at a stage where it is difficult to attempt to formulate generalisations at all, with any degree of certainty, apart from the need to see the dominant class in holistic terms (despite its acknowledged fractions) as opposed to seeing the dominant class in a structural sense of being a specific functioning group, in the fashion favoured by the radical structuralist framework of the dependency theorist in the mid-1970s.

To urge this holistic approach to the dominant class is not, however, to assert a relatively straightforward process of analysis of class formation in the Third World. Discussions of the nature of class formation and the role of the post-colonial state have specific 'levels of analysis' criteria which need to be applied. To talk about a dominant class that interacts with the international environment requires a different perspective to an analysis which focuses on that dominant class's domestic relationship within the specific social formation. In this latter context, the class frequently looks less dominant than it does when it is involved in a process of international interaction. As Hyden (1980) has recently demonstrated, some significant sections of the national community of Third World states have the ability to 'opt out', as for example in Tanzania where the dominant class has been unable to bring sections of the 'uncaptured peasantry' under its total control. In the Third World, classes are, on the whole, more complex (subdivided), weaker and incomplete (in the process of formation) than, for example, classes in advanced industrial society, and their behaviour is conditional on their interaction with other classes in a given social system at a given point in time (see Roxborough 1979: 72, 87-8).

As with class, then similarly with the role of the post-colonial state: we need to recognise the variety of stages of development and the subsequent range of options open. The post-colonial state is neither economically determinist nor politically voluntarist. The economic structure may well be the dominant factor, but it does not preclude the state, or rather the personnel of the state, behaving with varying degrees of political or ideological independence. The major pitfall that needs to be avoided in the attempts by students of underdevelopment to build up some kind of generalised hypotheses around the nature of the state in post-colonial societies is the danger inherent in the creation of one or possibly two abstract models of the 'state-in-general'. This pitfall has often not been avoided, especially by dependency theorists. It would seem methodologically absurd to make generalisations about the post-colonial state when our data and knowledge of its functioning in individual cases is almost always inferior to that which we possess about the advanced industrial state, but about which we are far less ready to make sweeping statements.

Concluding Remarks

By using a form of analysis comparable to that employed in the previous chapter, this chapter has portrayed the radical debate on underdevelopment that has evolved during the 1970s as a process approximating neither to a Popperian view of scientific development nor to a process of dialectical interchange. Rather should it be seen in a sociological sense as a process of encroachment or accretion. It is important, therefore, that the recent innovations should not be seen as a total undermining of dependency theory — or 'radical structuralism' or the 'sociology of underdevelopment', to give dependency theory its other names. It was suggested that dependency is a *syndrome* of charac-teristics extending beyond the 'development-of-underdevelopment' hypothesis; but at its inception, this hypothesis was clearly the centre of attention, a 'tour de force', and an exciting and energising con-ception when seen as a critique of modernisation theory. Its influence on a whole generation of scholars is shown by the length of the bib-liography attached to this book, most of which addresses itself in one way or another to the development of underdevelopment. It is perhaps hardly surprising, therefore, that early critiques of the development of underdevelopment had little *immediate* impact on its popularity. The time lag between the publication of the work of Laclau and Warren, and their subsequent attainment of seminal status for those wishing to criticise dependency theory, again testifies to the importance of historiographical analysis.

This time lag between the popular acceptance of a set of ideas and the subsequent development of the process of their critical evaluation is a common characteristic of the history of ideas. While the second of these two processes is intellectually the more rewarding, it is also — in terms of psycho-sociological assurance — the more frustrating. Such reassurance was not, however, the purpose of this chapter. If we con-clude, therefore, by reflecting on the state of radical theory at the end of the 1970s, then its prospects for securing broad-based theoretical explanation in its own right are not promising. While it has clearly provided us with the wherewithal to overcome many of the obstacles presented by the limited concerns of the public policy of development discussed in Chapter 2, radical theory also has been shown to have limitations. While it is not my intention to suggest in the next chapter that the resolution of our problems can be achieved by a synthesis of our two schools of thought reviewed to date, it is my intention to suggest that there is a set of issues our understanding of which is enhanced only by a utilisation of concepts emanating from both intellectual traditions.

4 THE SEARCH FOR COMMON GROUND: PUBLIC POLICY AND THE STATE IN THE THIRD WORLD

The preceding two chapters are essentially reconstructions of theoretical 'in-house' debates in political development studies. Such reconstruction is justified to the extent that these debates do have acknowledged influence, both negative and positive, over practitioners and policy-makers. As many have attested (see, for example, Packenham 1973 and Apter 1980), this nexus was particularly influential during the first phase of development studies, entrusted as it was with the task of delivering the expected goods engendered in that optimistic era following World War II. Many of the dramatis personae, be they economists, political scientists or whatever, took their tasks extremely seriously. They were not engaged purely, as some of cynical persuasion have suggested (Bauer 1981), in empire-building and self-aggrandizement — although in some cases this has, unfortunately, been the most tangible result. One aim of this book is to emphasise the relationship between theory and policy. It is appropriate, accordingly, that this chapter should address itself, in part at least, to the variety of policy implications, or lack of them, that emerge from the theoretical bodies of knowledge examined in Chapters 2 and 3.

What has become increasingly apparent over the first three decades of development theorising is that neither development nor under-development can any longer be thought of as the universal processes they were initially assumed to be by both modernisation and dependency theorists. Complex and multiple forms of capital accumulation and socio-political evolution in various peripheral social formations are now recognised as facts of life and attempts to build universal theories are seen as essentially ideologically determined.

The ideological components of various theoretical innovations are, of course, important. It was dependency theory's ideological offensive against modernisation theory that enabled us to comprehend modern-isation theory's normative assumptions. In like fashion the ensuing critiques of dependency theory helped, in turn, pick out *its* set of normative assumptions, and the methodologically similar underpin-nings that it shared with modernisation theory. As Henry Bernstein pointed out, dependency theory 'replicates the circularity of modern-isation models and is likewise expressed in a series of conceptual

polarities: developed/underdeveloped, metropolis/satellite, centre/
periphery, autocentric growth/extroverted growth, domination/
dependence' (Bernstein 1979: 94, but see also Taylor 1979: 92-8). The
end product of dependency theory may have been *under*development
as opposed to development, but it exhibited an almost identical unilinear determinism to modernisation theory.

As suggested in the last chapter, however, the fortunes of dependency
theory were to prove short-lived as it gave way to a counter-attack from
a modified modernisation theory and a Marxism, both of which rallied
to defend themselves. As ideal types, both modernisation theory and
Marxism *had* to refute the notion of *under*development. This defence
was carried out first at the theoretical level — by challenging the illog-
icality of the development of underdevelopment hypothesis (see Laclau
1971), and later at an empirical level — as both modernisation theorists
and Marxists fastened on to the phenomenon of the NICS as proof
positive of the possibility of capitalist industrialisation in the Third
World. Indeed, it took analysts some time, steeped as they were in the
mood of pessimism that engulfed development studies in the late 1960s
and early 1970s, to appreciate the political and ideological significance
of the high growth rates of the 1960s of states such as South Korea,
Taiwan, Hong Kong, Singapore and to a lesser extent the Philippines,
Brazil and several other Latin American states. In this context, the
world systems modifications of dependency theory (*pace* Wallerstein
and Amin), the analysis of associated dependent development (Cardoso
1973 and Evans 1979), the more orthodox Marxist critiques (Warren
1973 and 1980 and Kay 1975) and the resurrection of certain aspects
of theories of imperialism were all particularly important theoretical
innovations.

This utility extended beyond simple criticism of dependency theory
as part of a 'radical', 'in-house' debate. It also acted as a partial corrective to the more orthodox kinds of analysis examined in Chapter 2.
As none other than David Apter has noted:

the theoretical language of marxism, particularly the dynamics of
polarisation, dialectical process, class formation and conflict were
far more important than *mainstream* [my emphasis] political
analysts allowed ... I believe public choice theory is essential
and valuable especially for understanding democratic politics. But
it omits too much and especially the specifically negative consequences of development particularly of the sort which marxist and
neo-marxist theory has been concerned with (Apter 1980: 270-2).

In essence, what Apter was saying, and he needs to be applauded for it since it has not happened often, is that competing schools of thought, be they liberal-choice-based public policy or variants of neo-Marxism, do not do justice to the complexity of the development process on their own. There should be no exclusive claims made for one research programme. Modernisation theory clearly is not dead and the range of opinion within the radical school is, in one way, a sign of intellectual health, although its failure to attract the large institutional support comparable to that of modernisation theory in the late 1950s/early 1960s has to be noted. This lack of support has occurred notwithstanding the fact that there has been a tacit acceptance of the respectability of many of its central tenets by analysts of non-Marxist persuasion. Its failure to attract support is due in no small part to the pessimistic nature of many of its prescriptions, particularly its assertion of the futility of reformism on the one hand, accompanied by the lack of any prospect of substantive revolutionary change on the other. The weakness of radical prescriptiveness, in contrast to its much stronger diagnostic capability, has effectively left the field wide open for the more 'hard-nosed' public policy modifications of modernisation theory. In effect, the status of radical theory is that of an ineffectual coalition forming the 'official opposition' in a parliament controlled by a ministry operating a renovated public policy of development. As David Goldsworthy pointed out in regard to the radical school:

> the sort of literature we are considering embodies a kind of self denying ordinance when it comes to questions of prescription. Accordingly we must expect the main strength of dependency and other radical analyses of the new imperialism to lie in diagnosis (Goldsworthy, n.d.: 21).

Pietistic assertions of a need for revolutionary change and the abolition of the existing order are not policy prescriptions that are likely to appeal to existing governing groups in the Third World. These governing groups might be keen to restructure the existing international order in so far as such a policy is likely to enhance their power, but it is unrealistic to expect them to support a restructuring of the domestic order that would in essence, following Amilcar Cabral, ask them to 'commit suicide as a class' (Cabral 1969: 59). In many ways this situation encapsulates the essential dilemma for anyone writing about the Third World. Despite its sophisticated, situational analyses of 'what is wrong in the Third World', radical theory is always likely to play second fiddle to policy-making approaches which, by the limited nature of the questions they ask, are always going to prove more attractive to governing groups, or would-be governing groups, in the vast majority of Third World countries. Ruling groups, as suggested in Chapter 2, inevitably find the incrementalist nature of policy analysis of considerable comfort.

Is there then a deadlock between two approaches, one of which is concerned with fundamental restructuring, and one of which is concerned with improving existing systems?[17] The answer, probably, is 'Yes.' All the same, it cannot be sufficient to accept such a deadlock and to proceed severely within the limits of one's own research programme. A book which includes, and attempts to build upon, discussion of two such divergent approaches certainly incurs the risk of outraging members of both schools. But we must, at least theoretically, accept the possibility of organising analysis around a common set of concepts. Such is the task to which the rest of this chapter is devoted.

As a starting point it is possible to see a process of 'working down' from our early macro-assumptions of the first phases of development studies to a more specific micro-orientation. Such a trend is quite clearly apparent in *both* schools. Where early modernisation theory was macro-sociological, the more recent public policy approaches are more micro-economic in orientation. Where early radical theory was extremely macro-sociological — dependency theory's fetish for grand dichotomies differing little from that of modernisation theory's — more recent radical theory, especially analyses of the role of the state, the nature of class formation and class behaviour is both historically and geographically much more specific. Grand theory does in fact exhibit very little attraction for either of our two broad schools of thought at the beginning of the 1980s. The analysis of the way a variety of modes of production might articulate in a particular peripheral social formation has had the effect of concentrating the minds of radical theorists in a fashion similar to the effect of public policy approaches on modernisation theory. It is in this context that both schools of thought have something to offer. Historic and geographical specificity in their analyses have caused both schools to pay much more attention to the role of the state in the Third World over the last few years more than at any time over the previous twenty or so; presenting, perhaps for the first time, an area of common ground on which to compare and maybe even synthesise certain aspects of their approaches. Chapters 2 and 3 were not really comparing like with like, given the essentially different concerns of our two schools of thought. This need not, however, be the case at the beginning of the 1980s.

The State of the Art, or the Art of the State?

At long last there seems to be little disagreement amongst analysts of
any persuasion that they have to come to grips with the nature and
functions of the state in the Third World if they wish to understand the
basis of the policy-making process. The state is clearly back in vogue —
even within mainstream political science.[18] Since this has not been the
case for much of the post-World War II period, perhaps a brief recap
would appear in order.

Implicit, if not explicit, in Chapter 2 was the suggestion that the
political science of political development had paid little or no attention
to the role of the state and its institutional structures *per se*. Rather it
had concerned itself with psycho-sociological explanations of political
behaviour in the Third World and had treated the state largely in the
pluralist sense of 'neutral arbiter'. Such consideration that the state
did receive was at pains to point out the weakness of its numerous
institutions. It was from this starting point, in the hey-day of modernisation theory, that we saw the drift towards an emphasis on order and
political stability and the resultant need to bolster the state. With the
benefit of hindsight we can see that the role of the state did in fact
increase in the post-colonial period in the Third World. The major
problem was that political scientists were slow to recognise it, and not
only in the Third World but in the advanced industrial societies as well.
As Alfred Stepan has noted: 'Whilst almost everywhere the role of the
state grew, one of the few places it withered away was in political
science' (Stephan 1978: 3). As radicals would be quick, and correct, to
point out, this was not the case with their analysis. As suggested in
Chapter 3, if anything the reverse was in fact so; with perhaps too
great an emphasis on the role of the state at the expense of understanding other relevant variables in the political process. This was
especially the case during the hey-day of dependency theory with its
very unsophisticated initial formulations, although, again as suggested
in Chapter 3, this over-reaction called forth a series of more restrained
efforts at corrective analysis.

In a strange kind of way, however, we have a situation nowadays in
which both Marxists and non-Marxists have a similar view of the behaviour of the state in the Third World — albeit operating from a
different normative base and utilising different terminology. Both
schools recognise the fundamental role of the state in political and
economic activity. In many ways, the differences between public policy
analysts seeing the institutions of the state as vital for regime maintenance

and development and Marxists who see it as oppressive and the major expropriator of surplus are largely semantic and normative.

If, as Stepan in his recent study has shown, the state is much more interventionist in liberal theory than we often like to assume, then this is even more the case in developing countries. The prime example, as Stepan suggests, is Brazil — often thought to be the epitome of liberal capitalist economic development — but which exhibits a major degree of state involvement in 'almost all facets of the country's economic and especially social structure' (Stepan 1978: 9).

The basic liberal notion of the self-regulating nature of the state which permeated the early political science of political development is not found to the same extent in the more recent public policy approaches to political activity in developing countries. Modernisation theory's early search for psycho-sociological influences and pluralist political activity reduced greatly our ability to recognise significant political factors such as the potential for some autonomy on the part of the state. If we think back, for example, to the structural functional models set out in the first edition of Almond and Powell's *Comparative Politics* (1966), their emphasis was on the analysis of inputs (articulation, aggregation, communication, etc.) rather than such outputs as the coercive and regulatory capacities of the state. To his credit, however, even in those early days, Almond was able to recognise the shortcomings of such an approach (Almond 1966: 55). Yet this neglect of outputs at the expense of inputs did, unfortunately, manifest itself throughout the vast bulk of the literature influenced by the Social Science Research Council Committee on Comparative Politics (see Montgomery 1969). The analyses of the radical school provided some counter to these tendencies, but its influence in the 1970s was of a fairly limited nature. It does, however, provide the basis for some kind of coming together of analysis for the 1980s.

It is probably inevitable, and indeed reflected in the structure of this book, that analysis will continue to turn around the respective terminologies of our two broadly defined schools. This terminology sees one school focus on those ruling groups (elites) who are represented by, or who dominate, the policy-making processes of the state whilst the other school sees the institutions of the state dominated by those groups (classes) generated by the dominant mode of production (capitalism) in the particular social formation. A couple of issues do, however, provide common avenues for exploration and offer some prospect for greater understanding. The first area of analysis that offers hope is, I would suggest, that area of inquiry surrounding the relative autonomy of the state — until recently, but no longer, the more or less exclusive preserve of 'in-house' Marxist debates. The second area entails a closer examination of the 'organic corporatist' characteristics of the state rather than its traditional liberal or Marxist characteristics.

On the first issue, we are now in a position where we acknowledge that the activity of the state is neither as economically determinist (as in some of the more reductionist radical material) nor as politically voluntarist (as in some of the more extreme forms of policy analysis) as some observers would have us believe. In an invaluable refinement of the Marxist analysis of the autonomy of the state, a recent study by Eric Nordlinger (1981) provides an acute explanation of the very real capabilities for the relative autonomy of the democratic industrial state. Despite its focus on industrial society, Nordlinger's work has obvious parallels for the Third World state. He makes the point that democratic theory, and that body of policy studies literature that draws on democratic theory's intellectual traditions, is essentially 'societally constraint centred'. The traditional analysis of state–society relations, be they what Nordlinger calls pluralist, neo-pluralist, social-corporatist or even Marxist, emphasises the preponderance of a variety of societal factors inhibiting state autonomy. Marxism's position, he points out, is somewhat paradoxical, given its view of the state as the constrainted agent of the bourgeoisie (i.e. structurally/societally determined) which yet supposedly exhibits a relative autonomy. But of all the Western approaches to understanding the democratic state, Marxism (especially since the time of the celebrated Poulantzas–Miliband debates) has been the only approach to recognise any meaningful kind of state autonomy. It is for this reason that credit has to be given to Marxist analysis, in a historiographical essay such as this, for the refinement that has come about in our thinking due to its influence over the last decade.

Nordlinger presents a splendidly and rigorously argued analysis of why most societally oriented approaches underestimate the potential for the autonomy of the *democratic* state in the policy-making process and why consequent policy analysis over the last decade has developed an inadequate conception of the state — where they have not neglected its importance totally. Nordlinger's analysis has two important implications for this discussion of the state in developing countries. First, and as was suggested in Chapter 2, much of the public policy approach to politics in developing countries is essentially derivative from that policy-oriented literature that has come to dominate mainstream political science over the last decade. As such, it too is intellectually derivative from the societal constraint approach to the role of the state — the essence of which, to repeat, is an emphasis on the relative weakness of the state. These orientations have also been a major aspect of the recent public policy literature of developing countries. Drawing heavily on the work of the later SSRC volume (Binder *et al.* 1971) and Samuel Huntington (1968), they stress the basic institutional fragility and policy incapability of the Third World state.

The second inference we can draw from Nordlinger's work is what might be called 'normative reversal'. In modern democratic theory the societal constraint approach to state activity is largely supported. Indeed, it is seen as a cornerstone of modern democratic thought. On the other hand, much of the recent public policy of development is underpinned by a directly opposing normative stance. Emphasis is placed on the need to create strong centralised state institutions capable of control, regime maintenance and the orderly running of the policy-making process. More often than not processes of democratic accountability are ignored and societal constraints on state activity in developing countries are not to be applauded or encouraged, given their tendency to lead to political instability.

This normative reversal in the application of democratic thought to the Third World can, of course, be found also in quite a lot of the recent literature pertaining to the role of the modern industrial state. Particularly interesting from the point of view of this historiographical essay is Samuel Huntington's opposition to what he perceives as excessive societal constraints and growing demands of the modern industrial state (the USA). In his work for the Trilateral Commission (1975), Huntington returns to his old theme of the need for order and greater control by the state. The importance for us here is that the growing attention paid to the role of the state in the political and economic activity of society is not simply a phenomenon of the study of the Third World. Many scholars, of all persuasions, have recognised the problems also facing the modern industrial state. For example, conservatives ask if governments can go bankrupt and how they can deal with the problems of government overload (see Rose and Peters 1977 and Brittain 1975). Marxists and assorted radicals have turned their analyses to problems of legitimacy (Habermas 1976), fiscality (O'Connor 1973) or the contradictions between the modern industrial state's accumulation and legitimation functions (Wolfe 1977). Also party to these discussions have been those scholars, again of varying persuasion, who have searched for the growth of corporatism in the modern state (see, *inter alia*, Schmitter 1974; Winkler 1976; Panitch 1977 and 1980; and Cawson 1978).

The utility or otherwise of such analyses of the modern industrial state are not of direct relevance here, rather they are of secondary importance to the extent that they have had undoubted influence on the analysis of the Third World state — as with the work of Miliband and Poulantzas. Several works of late have suggested the utility of a corporatist perspective on the Third World state (see Stepan 1978; Evans 1979; Higgott 1983 and Higgott and Robison 1983 forthcoming). This is a second area that I would suggest is worthy of further analysis, following on from discussion of the need to recognise the possibility of some autonomy for the state.

In a recent major application of this approach to the state in Peru, Al Stepan operates within what we might call a corporatist perspective — although he refers to it as 'organic statism'. In Stepan's analysis, the state is strong, interventionist and exhibits a relative degree of autonomy (Stepan 1978: 26-40). Characteristic of such an approach as Stepan's is a high degree of concern for political stability, accompanied at times by the somewhat paradoxical tendency to radical intervention for the purpose of bringing about significant structural change to achieve some defined perception of the common good. The make-up of most Third World states more often than not approximates more closely to this organic/statist model than either a liberal/pluralist or Marxist conception of the state.

This would appear so for two reasons. First, the wherewithal for the operation of a pluralist system, in the classic North American sense of the word — namely competitive vertical functional groupings — is clearly missing in most Third World states. Also missing is a truly dominant class typical of Marxist analysis. The absence of groups capable of imposing on the state the kinds of societal constraints central to democratic analysis elaborated by Nordlinger, accompanied by the absence of a 'non-hegemonic class' comparable to Marx's bourgeoisie and of which the state is but an agent, must surely allow the state some degree of autonomy. The consequence is some kind of organic corporatism exhibiting certain characteristics fairly easily identifiable at a general level in most Third World states. Stepan, for example, points to the desire on the part of governments to construct 'parameters, rules and infrastructure of a market economy' (1978: 41), but where the degree of control of the economy and polity will deviate from the abstract model. The model may vary from a fairly traditional liberal-market economy with aggregate group activity on the one hand to a more controlled and planned economy approximating towards some kind of socialism on the other. As Stepan suggests, these are not exact models, but merely abstractions to which states, to a greater or less extent, may approximate.

The corporatist model consequently is capable of covering states as divergent as the newly industrialising nations of South-East Asia through to African states such as Kenya and the Ivory Coast. Deviation from the model, as Stepan goes on further to suggest, usually takes one of two forms, or in many cases a combination of these two forms. First, at the political level, there is a tendency to *over*-control. Second, at the economic level, there is a tendency to *under*-control. This creates a kind of authoritarian corporatism which cracks down hard on the large mass of a Third World state's population at the same time as it provides a fairly unfettered degree of freedom to that state's entrepreneurial groups. These characteristics are particularly apparent in those states which approximate economically to Cardoso's associated dependent development model (Cardoso 1973), and of which the above-mentioned South-East Asian NICS, Brazil and Venezuela would be some of the prime examples.

There is, of course, a strong link between most of the literature on corporatism and the tendency towards authoritarianism in the Third World. As Richard Falk has pointed out, this authoritarianism may be of either the left (Leninisation) or the right (Brazilianisation) (Falk 1979). In both, however, we see the existence of a coalition of rulers and technocrats operating the administrative apparatus of the state in what is now generally known as 'technocratic authoritarianism'. We do not have to subscribe to the somewhat extreme views of Issa Shivji concerning the existence of a bureaucratic bourgeoisie, discussed in Chapter 3, to accept that the major trend of the last decade has indeed been the increasing power of bureaucracies at the expense of other actors and institutions in the policy-making process (see Peters 1979: 342). The growth of bureaucracy has not, however, always been accompanied by a commensurate growth in government capabilities to implement its policy decisions. This is not, of course, for want of trying on the part of Third World governments but rather because many insurmountable obstacles impede their decision-making, or more importantly their decision-*implementing*, capabilities. Paramount amongst these obstacles are the availability of resources (broadly defined) or internal and external hindrances to policies — for example, the objections of potential international partners, on the one hand, or an inability of 'sell' or justify policies to the domestic constituency at which they are aimed, on the other.

Again, it is the coercive aspect of a Third World bureaucracy that is of crucial importance in this context. Too often, however, literature that has discussed the role of the bureaucracy in Third World countries has unfortunately exhibited a total neglect of the bureaucracy as part of the 'state' as a political actor (see, for example, Schumacher 1975). Above all, literature on Third World bureaucracies and the policy-making process tends to ignore the relationship between the state and the nature of class power. Conversely, most analyses of the state and class formation have tended to be largely sociological in character and have made little or no effort actually to investigate specific cases of decision-making and policy implementation. At the risk of overstatement, it has to be emphasised that the observer of the policy-making process in the Third World cannot afford to focus on the institutions or the *process* to the exclusion of that now very useful body of literature on class and class behaviour in the Third World. Similarly, radicals must concern themselves as much with the actual processes of government as with the sociological backdrop to these processes. It is in this respect that the work of the two schools of thought reviewed in this book prove clearly complementary. Sociological analysis and policy analysis are both needs of the most basic kind. This is especially so when the conventional wisdom of policy analysis, as we might intuitively expect, is that there are more obstacles than aids to the implementation of policy in the Third World (see, *inter alia*, Peters 1979; McHenry 1979; Grindle 1980 and 1981; and Killick 1980).

Obstacles to policy implementation are in many ways the other side of the coin that suggests a certain degree of autonomy for the state in the policy-making process. Perhaps one of the most basic problems we face at the level of understanding is that of achieving a proper perspective on the vast range of Third World cases that face us. The successful implementation of policy generally, however, is always going to be impeded by the different bases of social knowledge. This applies not only at the level of the application of Western-oriented theory to Third World situations in unadulterated form, but also when Western theory has been modified even to take account of a specific Third World situation. This is a problem that faces orthodox and Marxist theory alike. As Goran Hyden has pointed out with regard to coping with the peasantry in the Third World, for example, 'peasants cannot possibly be at the forefront on the route to modern society, as such a development is bound to be at their expense: Therefore it is only logical that peasants resist state policies' (Hyden, 1980: 16). Such are the dilemmas of policy makers in the Third World. Rationalist assumptions, be they from orthodox policy-makers or Marxist political leaders, are essentially bureaucratic and impersonal systems of rule-making and can expect to be met, in a vast majority of instances, by sentiments ranging from indifference to downright hostility. These sentiments are likely to prevail irrespective of whether policies are geared to help, influence, control or suppress the would-be targets of the particular policy at issue.

Control over their communities by Third World political leaders is not necessarily assured by either utilitarian or authoritarian incentives. Both Marxist and public policy approaches alike often tend to ignore the potentiality of certain segments of Third World communities to 'exit' or opt out of the political process, to use Albert Hirschman's (1970) now celebrated phrase (see also Lamb 1975). Perhaps the most recent treatment of the questionable control which dominant groups supposedly exercise over their populations in the Third World appears in Goran Hyden's excellent study of the relative power of certain sections of the Tanzanian peasantry *vis-à-vis* the central government. He shows how, in many ways, the state lacks the necessary control agencies to actually 'get at' the peasantry – protected as they are by what Hyden calls the 'economy of affection' and the residual elements of pre-modern cultural agencies. As Hyden points out, we cannot take it for granted that 'those who control the state also control the society' (1980: 29). The state may be powerful enough to ensure the continued interests of those who run it, but not always powerful enough to extend their domain over the rest of society as quickly as they might like.

While Hyden's analysis is a very useful addition to our understanding and may be appropriate to many parts of contemporary Africa, it is not necessarily appropriate to all areas of the Third World where the peasant may no longer be as well protected from the intrusions of the modern state. On the basis of a reading of the history of other areas of the world, it would not be unreasonable to expect the kind of 'peasant power' that Hyden alludes to in the Tanzanian context to diminish over time. The real utility of Hyden's work is the sense of perspective it imparts to our general assertions about the growing strength of the state in the Third World. Hyden points out, by implication, a problem common to both Marxist and orthodox would-be policy-makers – namely the vital need for control over all aspects of the state's productive processes, including the peasantry: 'development is inconceivable without a more effective subordination of the peasantry to the demands of the ruling classes' (Hyden 1980: 31).

'Development' is often not a sufficient spur for governments to achieve cooperation from the community. The relationship between governments and peasantries is not as utilitarian as we often automatically assume. The central administrative structures of many Third World states often have very little to offer the peasantries of their societies. It is for this reason that coercion is often a major element in the relationship between bureaucrats and peasants. This situation may well explain why much of the policy literature on development, concerned as it is with rational and efficient policy implementation, perceives as vital the need for elite stability and centralised administrative control. The upshot, intentional or not, is that this literature provides a blueprint for the tendency towards technocratic authoritarianism in the Third World. The basic aim of policy-makers is to close the 'exit option' from public-sector control for unreconstructed and dissident elements of Third World states. It is perhaps not surprising, therefore, that when utilitarian inducements or rationalist explanations fail to achieve the desired rates of cooperation, many governments turn with apparent ease to more authoritarian measures.

As the literature would suggest, peasant intransigence is possibly less forceful and easier to combat nowadays in Latin America (Migdal 1974) and Asia (Scott 1976) than in Africa (Hyden 1980), but the point about the need for government control in the Third World bears repeating, as does the point that this control is not axiomatic. Peasant power, in this essentially negative reactive sense, however, must not be confused with the prospect of greater peasant power in the positive or initiating sense. What emerges from our discussion on the role of the state in the Third World is that the major issue is not one of revolution or reform. The control of state power in the Third World by ruling groups may not be total, but it does allow most regimes to cope with discontent from below. Regime change in the Third World, be it in regimes of radical or conservative persuasion, is still more often than not the kind of elite circulation envisaged by the likes of Pareto than an upsurge from below envisaged in the more pietistic revolutionary literature that emerged on the Third World from the dependency school, or the pens of revolutionaries turned scholar in the 1960s (see, for example, Debray 1967 or Guevara 1969). Increasing peasant immiserisation in some parts of the Third World has not been accompanied by revolutionary upsurge. The coercive capabilities of the Third World state are clearly much greater than its capabilities in the areas of economic and social development and reform.

At the most basic level, the major research need is for a combining of the analysis of the institutional and formalist policy-making approaches with the very useful socio-economic analyses of the state in Third World societies as reflected in the literature of more radical persuasion over the last few years. Particularly needed is an appreciation of the Third World state's potential for autonomy as discussed in the post-dependency refinements of authors such as Leys, Roxborough and Evans (see Chapter 3) and Nordlinger, discussed earlier in this chapter. The synthesis of these approaches gives us a much more plausible balance with regard to the potential activity of the state in the Third World when contrasted with the early reductionism characteristic of the hey-day of dependency theory. These reductionist views and the subsequent rigid class solidification and revolutionary action which much dependency theory envisaged have been shown to be totally inappropriate. Somewhat surprisingly for many observers, no doubt, the more constrained Marxist analyses of the balance between the autonomy of the state on the one hand, and the societal constraints envisaged in Nordlinger-type analyses on the other, have turned out to be much more appropriate interpretations of political forms and events in the contemporary Third World.

We are thus able to recognise two essentially different spheres of operation. Nascent national bourgeoisies in the Third World are quite clearly concerned to use the power of the state in any conflict between their own interests and those of intrusive foreign interests. Further, as Leys in his work on Kenya (1978) and Evans in his work on Brazil (1979) have demonstrated, national ruling groups have met with some considerable success in using the apparatus of the state in this manner. At the domestic level, ruling groups in the Third World are also keen to use the apparatus of the state for the preservation of their position *vis-à-vis* recalcitrant groups within society. In this context the degree of success, depending on other state capabilities, has been somewhat more mixed — as was indeed noted in the last chapter.

Discussion in this chapter has so far been concerned primarily with the status of the theoretical debate over the role of the state in the contemporary Third World setting — and these issues have been approached from an essentially political direction. There have, however, been changes in other aspects of development studies of a magnitude comparable to those that have taken place in the political science of political development and of which we must take notice in order to put our analysis into some kind of proper perspective. Particularly influential has been the so-called crisis in development economics. This crisis has, however, been much better documented than that in political science (see, *inter alia*, Nafziger 1980; Seers 1979; Leaver 1979; Streeton

1980). Suffice it here to say that while the political science of political development was evolving into a public policy of development as described in Chapter 2, development economics underwent a similar transformation. Rostovian optimism, accompanied by the international equivalent of a Keynesian welfare-state, diffusion process, gave way to a pessimism which saw some of the world's leading development economists prophesying the death of development economics (see Seers 1979).

The intellectual process in development economics was very similar to that which took place elsewhere. The essential weaknesses of development economics were also exposed by what we might call the structuralist critique outlined in Chapter 3. At the heart of this critique was the growing popularity of the primacy of notions of 'unequal exchange' at the expense of the orthodoxy of the previous hundred and fifty years — namely the doctrine of comparative advantage. During the brief hey-day of dependency theory, unequal exchange held sway. However, the rallying that we have seen by Marxist and orthodox theories in the political domain has also occurred in the economic domain. The policy implications of dependency theory in economic theory would appear, with the benefit of hindsight, to be as absurd as its views of the role of the state posited in much of the literature of the mid-1970s. At a policy prescriptive level, the implications of dependency theory and world systems theory are not to be taken seriously. Their view of the world system as the only meaningful level of analysis trivialises everything that takes place at the state, regional and sub-regional levels in a way, that to their credit, neither of our two counters to dependency do; particularly in their more *specific* emphasis on the post-dependency era.

The long-term expectation of world systems theory is, of course, that the capitalist world system will collapse at some unspecified time in the future. In the meantime, the logical prescription of this approach, with its unequal exchange rejection of comparative advantage, even if only implicitly stated, is withdrawal from the world market. Both Marxist and orthodox development theory has articulated quite forceful arguments to suggest that such a policy prescription is not a possible consideration for Third World states, be they of capitalist or socialist inclination. Dependency theory was impractical in a further sense. It offered no suggestions for how a state pursuing such policies of closure could achieve them and still obtain the necessary commodities, be they material, scientific or technological, that can only be obtained from the world market. Yet, while dependency theory cannot be, and indeed is not, taken seriously at the policy level, it is incorporated quite extensively at a rhetorical level into the language of Third World politics, especially in that crude kind of 'Third Worldism' which allows both left and right to join together in condemnation of the exploitation of the periphery by the core. It is in this context that demands for the creation of a New International Economic Order, as the only possible remedy for the problems facing developing countries, echo from many ruling groups in Third World countries with a very hollow ring.

To make such criticisms is not, however, to question the importance of world systems analysis. In the succinct words of Fred Cooper:

> The problem is that dissecting complex problems with concepts like underdevelopment, incorporation, unequal exchange and core-periphery relations is rather like performing surgery with an ax: the concepts cut, but messily. What is needed is a fuller discussion of what is systematic about the world system, and that means more sensitive theoretical and empirical examinations of distinct types of capital, their development and interrelation; of the flow of credit and investment — International Monetary Fund and multinational corporations; of commercial organisations; of states; and of the often contradictory ways that the specific classes react and adapt to changing opportunities and constraints in world markets (Cooper 1981: 16).

As in political science, then so in economics, the outcome of the reaction to the inadequacies of dependency theory has been a reversion to political economy of a more restrained and policy relevant nature. At the core of this political economy is the notion of 'urban bias' in the Third World and the way this bias ensures that wealth transfers to the Third World go to the better-off incumbent urban elites rather than trickling down to the rural poor. As the leading exponent of the urban bias thesis has pointed out:

> the 60 to 80% of the people dependent on agriculture are still allocated barely 20% of public resources . . . So long as the elite's interests, background and sympathies remain predominantly urban, the countryside may get the priority but the city will get the resources (Lipton 1977: 17-18).

Lipton's thesis owes much to the notions of 'cumulative inequality' and 'circular causation' thwarting trickle down and preventing spread effects. These ideas had, as is well known, been articulated by Gunnar Myrdal as early as 1957. The recent policy outcome of the acceptance of the influence of urban bias has been a growing advocacy of Redistribution with Growth (RwG) strategies and Basic Needs programmes in the Third World — these policies came to be epitomised in the mid-1970s literature of such bodies as the World Bank and the Institute of Development Studies (see, *inter alia*, Chenery *et al.* 1974 and Ul Haq 1976).

The successful implementation of such policies does, however, pose several interesting, if not embarrassing, questions for our analysis of policy-making and the role of the state as outlined in the earlier sections of this chapter. If the people in rural areas are poor because they are starved of resources by inhabitants of the urban areas, then how is this process to be reversed? Since the market cannot guarantee the delivery of the required resources, redirection can only come about by the intervention of the state to ensure a process of enforced trickle down. On the basis of the marginal evidence available to date, Redistribution with Growth would in fact seem to be one of the few ways of alleviating the lot of the rural poor, to whatever minimal level, in the Third World (see George 1976: 64-5). Yet, the prospects for successful implementation of such policies in the Third World on any major scale do not appear encouraging, especially in the light of relationships between dominant groups and the policy-making process. The essential ingredient for the success of RwG strategies is *political will* on the part of ruling groups in Third World states since it is they who are, in essence, asked to redistribute their political and economic power (such as it is) away from themselves.

Such a course of action would appear unlikely on at least two counts. First, as Leaver has suggested, albeit in terms somewhat more restrained than Amilcar Cabral's (cited earlier): 'the necessary reforms involve the self-immolation of all neo-classical elites' (1979: 4); and, as suggested in Chapter 2, the predominant policy-making models are geared to upholding and reinforcing elite authority in the Third World in a manner inconsistent with such reformist strategies. Second, again as suggested in Chapter 2, the 'mobilisation of bias' in the policy-making process — particularly the disparities in power between the illiterate and poor rural populations by contrast to that of the centralised governing groups — minimises the prospect of altering this balance through pressure from below. Public-policy analysis, stressing elite maintenance, is not — as Mahbub Ul Haq has suggested (1976:

24ff) — likely to encourage direct attempts to alleviate rural poverty. Such would appear to be the case under both capitalist and socialist models of economic development. Capitalist roads to development require high injections of capital, the acceptance of significant income inequalities and the preservation of these inequalities for elite satisfaction. Socialist alternatives in many ways pose similar dangers, particularly the tendency towards heavy bureaucratisation that inevitably accompanies those kinds of regimes. To attack poverty requires a political will not characteristic of bureaucratic and technocratic decision-making. In this context there is a clear distinction between policy and administration. Efficient planning and administration are futile in a situation where the political will to restructure the politico-economic balance is lacking. The probability for major success for RwG strategies would, therefore, seem strictly limited.

The distinct reluctance with which RwG proposals are greeted by the majority of the Third World's political elites has to be contrasted, as I suggested earlier, with the popularity of demands for a redistribution at the international level under the guise of demands for a New International Economic Order. It is neither necessary, nor indeed possible, to review here the vast body of literature (much of which is of very poor quality) on the NIEO.[19] It is, however, worth pointing out the clear link that exists between certain broad themes in development thinking and the emergence of the NIEO movement over the last decade. The intellectual influences on these calls are in fact quite easily traced. They date back to the ECLA's initial objections to the asymmetrical nature of the world economy in the late 1950s, through the creation of UNCTAD in 1964, the Pearson Report of 1969, the UN Declaration on the Establishment of a New International Economic Order in the mid-1970s through to the publication of the Brandt Report in 1980 and most recently the Cancun summit in October 1981. Politically, the concept of the NIEO was an idea 'whose time had come' in the mid-1970s and it had quite clear intellectual debts to the influence of the structuralist/dependency theories of that period. Similarly, the eclipsing of dependency theory in recent years is also reflected in the attitudes of policy-makers concerning North/South development issues. In fact, attitudes towards calls for a New International Economic Order are perhaps as good a litmus test as any to identifying the competing perceptions of the Third World development process encompassed in any particular school of thought.

In a quite masterful analysis of the literature of the North/South Dialogue and the New International Economic Order, Robert Cox

(1979) outlined what he perceived as the five major 'opinion clusters' of attitudes towards these issues. They involve an 'establishment' view emanating from the major industrialised countries and epitomised in the views of the Trilateral Commission (see Sklar 1980) in the second half of the 1970s and the views of the Reagan administration in the first half of the 1980s; second, a 'social democratic' perspective found in the work of the Institute of Development Studies, the International Labour Organisation and the Club of Rome (see Tinbergen 1976); third, what we might call the official Third World view, represented by the Mahbub Ul Haq (1976) and UNCTAD positions on the New International Economic Order; and, finally, two slightly less satisfactory, 'mercantilist' categories embodied, on the one hand, in the work of Robert Tucker (1977) and perhaps more recently in that of Peter Bauer (1981), and, on the other, a 'historical materialist' category, together that whole gamut of authors reviewed in some detail in Chapter 3 of this book. The great value of Cox's work is that it highlights quite specifically the relationship that exists between theory and practice in the development industry.

For the purposes of this chapter, the major issue is what may be referred to as the almost total eclipse of the 'development—of underdevelopment' hypothesis at the centre of dependency theory. 'Dependence' as a concept is still very important, but in a way that has been portrayed by Tony Killick as the difference between what he sees as the 'dependency theorists' and the 'dependency worriers'. At the policy level, the theorisers see any kind of 'piecemeal reform as futile' (Killick 1980: 383), whereas dependency worriers have in fact had a good deal of influence on policy, particularly in advocating, for example, tougher bargaining with MNCs and 'more self-reliant development strategies; export diversification, redistributive measures; and that group of proposals labelled NIEO' (Killick 1980: 383). This genre of literature emanates quite clearly from our more orthodox stream of liberal political economy and would appear at this point to occupy a fairly central position amongst development theorists. The central thrust of this position is a reassertion of the utility of comparative advantage as a workable empirical concept *vis-à-vis* the short-lived ascendancy of unequal exchange. This position is put most forcefully in a recent work by Hollis Chenery (1979). While Chenery questions, in highly critical fashion, some of the classical assumptions of comparative advantage, he does, nevertheless, demonstrate its continued utility. This is particularly so in assessing the relative merits of export promotion *vis-à-vis* import substitution industrialisation policies in the Third World.

The importance of Chenery's analysis is not that it totally refutes notions of unequal exchange, but that it alerts us to the complexity of the Third World situation. As such it undermines further, if that is still necessary, the *all embracing nature* of the initial development–of– underdevelopment hypothesis and its policy advocacy of withdrawal from the world system of trade. Complexity must be our watchword. The evidence of the last decade is precisely that some states benefit greatly from incorporation whilst other states quite clearly do not. As such, efforts to build general theory in economic development have met with the same derisory success, as have similar efforts in political science. The major sign of hope is probably the recognition by both disciplines of the importance of their work for each other. Particularly important has been the acceptance by economists that the implementation of economic policies is not simply a technical issue. It is much more readily acknowledged nowadays by economists just how significantly market behaviour can be overridden by political decisions (see Almond and Genco 1977). Technical innovation, at some stage or another, comes up against political forces, the suppression of which is usually a prerequisite for a different evolutionary path – of whatever direction. Whether a government is genuinely interested in the improvement of the levels of mass welfare or simply intent on preserving its own position, it is, nevertheless, the political parameters that are ultimately crucial to its success or failure.

In contemporary Third World politics today, the national state, as the junction between the domestic and international levels of action, is the principal arena of political activity. As I have tried to suggest in this chapter, it is from the level of the central state in the Third World that the policy-making process is initiated and controlled, or not, as the case may be. In consequence, I have also suggested the *naïveté* of a form of analysis which tries to understand the policy-making process emanating from this level purely from within the purview of one school of thought. An understanding of the role of the state in the Third World demands not only a cognisance of the socio-economic structural position of its institutions and personnel, but also analysis of the actual processes of policy-making and policy implementation within these broader structures. At the risk of repetition and overstatement, we may conclude by saying that neither the public policy of development nor radical theory is sufficient in itself: each needs to take the other seriously.

CONCLUSION

It has become apparent — with the benefit of hindsight — that under-standing the problems and dilemmas of the developmental process is really much easier than prescribing for their resolution at the policy level, or attempting to build general theoretical models from which policy can be deduced. Such a recognition notwithstanding, we do not have to retreat to an extreme position, such as that espoused by the conservative, Peter Bauer:

> There is no Third World development problem. Rather there are innumerable societies with widely differing conditions of life and expectations for the future.... The so called Third World develop-ment problem was created by those who lumped together the innumerable societies of the Third World (Bauer 1981: 143).

Nor need we side with the Marxist economic anthropologists who, to paraphrase Aiden Foster-Carter, discover a new mode of production in every new Andean valley they visit (Foster-Carter 1978). Both positions are essentially extremist: they deny entirely the commonality of many Third World problems and situations; and they reject the undeniable ideological unity that is *perceived* in the Third World as having a bear-ing on all Third World states. It is irrelevant that this Third World 'identity' is essentially a fabrication of political elites, as indeed analysts close to Professor Bauer's position have pointed out (see Harries 1979). But having said all this, we also need to avoid what Hirschman called 'compulsive and mindless theorising' (1970: 329) which to a large extent epitomised early modernisation theory and dependency theory.

It is unlikely that there will be, and indeed it is possible to argue that there should not be, one dominant paradigm. It is misguided to expect the emergence of a single theory. Blueprints for change are essentially political phenomena, not theoretical ones. It is consequently important to spell out our normative assumptions at the outset. The failures of the first two development decades make normative concerns all the more important, especially since we have retreated from the initial positions we occupied at the beginning of this period. The notion of progress as the advance from an inferior past to a superior future and the inevitablity of this process is no longer taken for granted —

particularly in advanced industrial societies, where most of the theory which we have been reviewing comes from (see Nisbet 1980: 9). This waning faith is manifested in several forms. Economically, it is manifested in growing scepticism about the prospects of continued economic growth (see especially Meadows *et al.* 1972). Similar fears have been expressed regarding the *social* limits on growth (see Hirsch 1977). Politically, numerous authors have expressed their doubts about the continued viability of democracy (see Huntington *et al.* 1975). At a general level, this waning faith in advanced industrial societies is part and parcel of the similar attitudes adopted towards the prospect for development in the Third World. Both are a reflection of the retreat from the certainty concerning our ability to deal with the problems of society in a rational and technical fashion which dominated Western social and political thought only two decades ago.

Particularly in the Third World, pressures to modernise have brought with them accompanying pressures undreamt of by early theorists. The recognition of the finite nature of resources, be they social or economic, and accompanying pressures for redistribution have done much to undermine the consensual basis that was supposed to underpin the social and political theory of the immediate post-World War II period. The non-consensual basis of much contemporary political behaviour is nowhere better illustrated than in the North—South confrontation between the haves and have-nots of world society. In this context it is, for once, difficult not to agree with Peter Bauer when he suggests that reports such as Brandt (1980) are not, as its subtitle would imply, 'Programmes for Survival' but rather 'signposts to political conflict' (Bauer 1981: 140).

Such gloomy prognostications are not to imply that things have not changed significantly in the Third World in the post-World War II period. Indeed, there have clearly been quite dramatic transformations in certain parts of the Third World, as we now recognise with regard to the emergence of the NICs. Radicals in the hey-day of dependency theory, on the one hand, were reluctant to acknowledge what we might in popular parlance call the 'South-East Asian miracle'. Orthodox development theorists, on the other hand, wearing the rose-tinted glasses of modernisation theory, were reluctant to acknowledge the essentially lop-sided, and often brutal, nature of this development. The deductive nature of both schools of thought, seated in their Western intellectual tradition, prevented them in the first instances from asking serious questions about local prevailing conditions in the Third World. Even to this day, most analysts of the developmental process — be they conservative, radical or whatever, tend to internalise the literature of their own particular genre or discipline before they proceed to their own research. Further, most policy-makers from the Third World pass, at some stage or other, through the tertiary institutions of advanced societies, where they internalise much of this Western intellectual tradition — or what Hyden (1980) calls 'trained incapacity'.

If we reflect on this internalisation process that most Third World policy-making elites go through, we can see that it is an almost entirely opposite process to that of would-be *recipients* of development policies on the ground in the Third World. As Goran Hyden has perceptively pointed out, most policy-makers in the Third World

> promote images of the peasants as willing collaborators with government. On such an assumption they are usually able to sell their agricultural development policies to those who provide finance. Western socialists often engage in a similar approach. In the context of their theory, the peasants are revolutionary and the bourgeoisie the main stumbling block to a more far reaching transformation of society. Most of this is wishful thinking, if not downright ignorance (Hyden, 1980: 211).

We do not have to go as far as does Hyden in his analysis of the obdurate nature of the peasantry in Tanzania to recognise the implications of his analysis for a public policy of development emanating from a Western, especially systems-based, intellectual tradition. Such a form of analysis might well 'fit', superficially at least, a Third World bureaucracy staffed by Western-trained university graduates. It would, however, appear most inappropriate in a rural setting where the influence of central government diminishes almost in proportion to the distance one gets away from the administrative centre. Yet, public and rational-choice-based theories of public policy seem to be gaining increasing attention of late (see, for example, Russell and Nicholson 1981 and Bates 1981). Will the application of such models in the Third World, despite their presently fashionable image in advanced industrial society, produce yet another instance of 'trained incapacity'? While such models clearly have some utility, we should be extremely cautious about transferring them in wholesale fashion to Third World contexts. Again, to quote from Hyden's very perceptive analysis, when we utilise those forms of analysis underpinned by the premiss of

> methodological individualism there is great danger of evolving

irrelevant policy advice. This approach tries to explain collective decision making as primarily the summation of different, individual decisions made separately. To be rational in that model implies the ability to see every relevant experience as a problem which can be broken into parts, reassembled, manipulated in practical ways and measured in its effects. Man is 'economic man' in the sense that he allows himself to be guided by priorities and tastes as expressed in the market. In his efficiency calculus, he comes to treat essentially economic variables as the tangible and quantifiable factors in society. The rest are reduced to the status of 'externalities' (Hyden 1980: 313).

In such a situation, other non-quantifiable, or less quantifiable, factors tend to be downgraded or simply ignored. This *might* not be such a fundamental problem in the advanced industrial context where market forces are highly developed — though this proposition too would be questioned by many — but it is a problem of the first magnitude in a Third World context. At this point, systems-based or rational-choice-based theories of policy-making — especially to the extent that they are devised in contexts isolated from the structural and cultural realities of the Third World experience — must be treated in very sceptical fashion. 'Economic rationality' and 'efficiency' are not the only variables taken into account by Third World populations when making economic decisions (I am not of course suggesting that they are irrelevant). Other factors such as kinship, religion or satisfactional and recreational aspects of the outcome of a particular decision can be of equal importance.

In similar fashion to these cautionary remarks about the influence of rational-choice theory on policy-making, there are a couple of points that need to be made with regard to the influence of organisation theory — particularly Weberian views pertaining to the nature of bureaucratic organisation. While most Third World bureaucracies are undoubtedly derived from Western bureaucratic models and staffed by graduates of Western universities, residual non-bureaucratic influences still play a major role — with obvious implications for the utility of Western-derived policy-making approaches. Further, a brief examination of the attitudes of the recipients of policy — people on the receiving end of the formal organisational structure — appears to show that this structure, where it is not received with blanket hostility, is often deemed to have little or no relevance. Most rural societies of the Third World operate within their own institutional frameworks, which are no less influential over the policy-making process for not being able to be fitted into a formal organisational model. This of course will vary from state to state and region to region within a particular state to the extent that the productive processes and structures of that region have been penetrated by the economic and political forms of advanced industrialism.

Perhaps an important point to note is that the policy-making process is just as likely to be impeded by the inapplicability of such models under either supposedly capitalist or socialist structures and regimes in the Third World. Efficiency and rationality permeate the work of Marx and those who purport to follow his guidelines just as much as it permeates the work of Max Weber and derivatives from his models. 'Socialists' cannot dodge such issues by dismissing them as the product of 'bourgeois' or 'positivist' thought. Alternative development strategies of the *Small is Beautiful* (Schumacher 1974) variety also tend to miss the point. As suggested earlier in this chapter, most Third World governments are preoccupied with attempting to gain proper control of their policy-making systems at the national administrative level rather than trying to bring about a devolution of administrative structures to local and regional levels. Calculations of rationality and efficiency often have little or nothing to do with processes which are seen essentially in 'power political' terms. As Hyden has suggested, 'small is powerful' (Hyden 1980: 213), not beautiful. As such it is to be mistrusted and thwarted as part of that process of consolidation of the centralised state.

These models — be they 'capitalist', 'socialist' or 'alternative' — are, more often than not, offered up for implementation by professional analysts from the industrial world who have no direct assumption of responsibility for the political implications or eventual outcomes of their advice. While it is certainly appropriate to include Western Marxists for criticism in this context, it must be an issue of greater concern *vis-à-vis* the contemporary public policy of development. The growth of policy studies over the last decade, and the greater congeniality of its advice to incumbent Third World regimes — especially concerning regime stability and elite maintenance — has given such studies an increasingly influential voice in the Third World policy-making process. A primary, or even a secondary, focus on regime maintenance inevitably means that research will focus on problems from the perspective of a particular regime and the domestic and international bureaucracies that service it.

There would appear to be an interesting, but disappointing, parallel

here between the earlier and later stages of post-World War II development theory. A characteristic of early theory-building, and policy
application, was the deductive manner in which study of the Third
World simply extrapolated from the literature and analysis of advanced
industrial society. This assertion holds good, I think, whether we are
talking about the way we adapted the work of Parsons, Rostow, Kindleberger or the major democratic theorists just as much as if we talk
about the way in which some of the literature on Soviet industrialisation was adapted for Third World conditions — perhaps the prime
example in this context being Paul Baran's *Political Economy of
Growth*. In these later, though still infant, stages of development
studies, it would appear that the process is repeating itself. Much of
the public policy of development, as Chapter 2 went to some lengths
to demonstrate, is simply extrapolation from the burgeoning body of
literature within mainstream political science and embraced by the
generic name of 'policy studies'. It would be a great pity if we did not
learn from the mistakes of the first generation of development studies.
It is in its utility as part of a potential learning process that I offer this
historiographical analysis of recent political development.

Learning from Historiographical Analysis

Historiographical analysis is primarily a negative activity, concerned
as it is with the past. It is also a rather smug activity — it is always easier
to be wise after the event than to appreciate fully the implications of a
particular mode of analysis as it is actually in train. I would like to
suggest, however, that at a basic level it provides greater comprehension of complex bodies of knowledge. Yet more than that, by weighing
up what has gone before, we can get some insight into the way things
might develop and, in a more normative fashion, the way we might like
things to develop in the future. Chapter 4 in fact suggests that our
previous attempts to analyse the role of the state in the Third World
should have set the scene for future analysis of a slightly more sophisticated form. In similar, albeit more general, vein it will be in order to
make several general suggestions about the two major areas of literature
reviewed in this book. It may be worth repeating that there are essentially only *two major* perspectives in development studies since World
War II. Just as Marx did not deny the existence of other classes than the
bourgeoisie and the proletariat, I do not deny the existence of other
perspectives on development. I simply wish to suggest that they are not

of particular moment.

Looking at the political science of political development as a case study of modernisation theory, I have suggested that there was a shift to what we might call a 'policy' approach by the end of the 1970s. Chapter 2 portrayed such a trend as the outcome of both continuity and change: *continuity* in that the current public policy of development clearly has intellectual origins in modernisation theory and in that it borrows from the significant work of early scholars such as Almond, Apter and Easton and the 'order'-dominated work of the SSRC Committee on Comparative Politics; *change*, in that it is a reaction to the grand theorising of modernisation theory. The new political economy and the subsequent public policy approaches, in their emphasis on economics, choice and decision-making, clearly represent a strong reaction to the heavy sociological emphasis of the 1960s.

The other major aspect of the reaction to modernisation theory has been in the demand for relevance. But this has, in many ways, had the effect of reinforcing modernisation theory rather than totally negating it. Because of its diffuse and descriptive character, modernisation theory failed to develop an empirically based problem-solving orientation that could provide a framework for analysis. In many ways, therefore, the growth of a public policy approach to development has been an exercise in making relevant the major aspects of modernisation theory policy. The focus on public policy has thus provided continuity in that it provides a way of 'managing' and administering the diffusion of aid, technology and cultural rationality and of ensuring the creation and support of Western-oriented decision-making elites.

Equally important has been the determination of this school not to opt, in all but minimal fashion, for the hypotheses and modes of analysis of the radical genre of literature on underdevelopment that has proliferated over the last decade and that was reviewed in Chapter 3. While we have come back to some of the central questions about power — of the 'who-gets-what-how-and-at-the-expense-of-whom' variety — there has been little concerted effort to extend these questions to the international relationships between the haves and have-nots of world society, or to the role that the state and class formation might play in these relationships.

It is in these aspects of Third World studies that the radical genre of literature has made its contribution over the last decade — but in similar fashion to modernisation theory, largely to the exclusion of other concerns. It too, however, has undergone a process of sophistication and refinement from the early days of dependency theory.

Particularly influential has been the desire of Marxists to undermine the 'development-of-underdevelopment' hypothesis, with its accompanying negative view of capitalism in the Third World. In many ways, Marxists have achieved this task very comfortably. The credibility of more classical approaches to imperialism such as those of Luxemburg and Lenin have reasserted themselves quite forcefully over the initial dependency conceptualisation. Capitalism has been given its rightful emphasis as a mode of production as well as a system of exchange, not *simply* a system of exchange (see Warren 1980 and Brewer 1980). Balance is, however, as much a problem for the Marxist as it is for the modernisation theorist. Radical analysis exhibits a precarious tendency to swing from macro-analytical theorising about the process of circulation on a world scale on the one hand, to a micro-analytical discussion of modes of production in specific, peripheral social formations on the other (see Foster-Carter 1978).

So what can we learn from historiographical analysis? Clearly, the central tenets of the modernisation and Marxist research programmes still remain. They have proved themselves to be, as suggested in Chapter 1, 'good swimmers' and have reasserted themselves against the short-lived popularity of dependency theory — or at least the raw dependency theory so popular in the mid-1970s. In some ways it is difficult not to feel sorry for dependencia approaches to development. They have been caricatured, or set up as straw men, in order to be laid to rest. The *Institute of Development Studies Bulletin* went through this funereal process in 1980 (Godfrey 1980: 4), as did the United States African Studies Association, somewhat belatedly, in October 1981 (see, *inter alia*, Cooper 1981; Sklar 1981; and Lofchie 1981). Such gratuitous judgement in many ways represents a failure to recognise the very sophisticated process of transfiguration attained by some of the initial protagonists of dependencia theory in Latin America on their own (see especially Cardoso 1973).

Indeed, Chapter 3 of this book is not entirely above the charge of caricaturing dependency theory. My excuse is that it is necessary from the historiographical point of view to highlight the extremely important role the more populist Frankian expositions of the development—of—underdevelopment hypothesis played in providing the necessary springboard from which both orthodox and Marxist theoreticians could leap through into the next phase of their intellectual development. While this book is critical of dependency theory, it has not meant to belittle its more important achievements, not the least of which was restoring 'political economy' to its rightful place centre stage in the social sciences. That it was 'poor political economy', as Nove (1974) was keen to tell us, was really only of secondary consideration in the first instance as was the fact that there is no really dominant approach to contemporary political economy. For while 'we might all be political economists nowadays', all political economists are certainly not the same. As we have seen, the 'public policy of development' has grown out of the resurgence of political economy, stressing rational-choice theory, allocation and the maximisation of decision-making capabilities. On the other hand, 'radical' political economy has been nurtured upon a strange diet of radical structuralism and historical materialism, stressing the importance of circulation and exchange (initially) and (more recently) productionism.

Judging by the current concerns of both research programmes, there is some consensus as to the important issues for analysis. If this is not openly acknowledged, it is at least implicit in the fact that both research programmes study (despite differing terminology) the ruling group — whether called the 'decision or policy-making elite' or the 'ruling or dominant class'. Similarly, both research programmes are, as suggested, much more historically and spatially specific. There is also a growing tendency for more mainstream political science to recognise the importance of the international connection, although referring to dependence or interdependence (see Duvall and Freeman 1981) as opposed to neo-colonialism and imperialism. Both programmes, of course, reject the notion of dependency in its original 'underdevelopment' form. The major areas of common research — elaborated upon in the previous chapter — concern the role that the state plays and should play and the issue of authoritarianism. Essentially, both research programmes ask a common, multifaceted question, i.e.: 'How can the creation and redistribution of assets and opportunities be achieved and under what kinds of control or coercion mechanisms?' Clearly, we should seek some middle ground between the extremes of one research programme viewing authoritarianism simply as the outgrowth of specific cultural tendencies in a society (for example values, roles and psychological factors), often justifying it at the policy level as necessary for 'stability' and 'development', while the other sees it as the consequence of the specific historical development of a set of social and economic relations of production. It is possible and necessary to combine some kind of socio-cultural analysis of tradition — at which analysis much modernisation theory is so adept — with an approach that stresses the impact of international processes of circulation and production on developing countries. For such a synthesis to occur, however, several things need to happen.

Modernisation theorists and public policy analysts have to confront several questions. Do classes exist? Is there such a thing as a mode of production? Is imperialism a serious concept? Should they decide that economic and class factors are of significance in explaining political forms and conflicts, the nature of the relationship between these factors will have to be expressed in more general and theoretical terms than they often are, and then examined in specific historical contexts. It is only by a sustained rejection of the utility, even in limited form, of these concepts, that an approach which stresses short-term incrementalism — with its emphasis on regime stability, elite maintenance and the degree and efficiency of the state/bureaucratic apparatus — can have any normative justification.

For political economists of radical persuasion, the major problem would appear to be that of forgetting (for a time at least) their dual obsessions with developing a general theory of the state and examining the specific historical development of political forms and conflicts around what, in many ways, appear the analytically unworkable concepts of mode of production and social formation. It would seem methodologically absurd to make generalisations concerning the nature of the state in the Third World when our data and knowledge of its functioning in individual cases is almost always inferior to that which we possess about the advanced industrial state, but about which we are far less ready to make sweeping generalisations. Above all, the question of the autonomy of the cultural and the political levels *vis-à-vis* the economic has to be confronted in the Third World context. Consequently, the radical political economist may properly be urged to resist the temptation to throw out the modernisation baby with the bathwater. A modernisation framework can very often highlight the connections between changes within sections of specific societies, especially when those changes are socio-cultural in nature and internally generated (see Grew 1980 and Smith 1976). In general, we need to make a conscious attempt to situate in as common a theoretical framework as possible, cultural, political, social and economic aspects of the production processes in specific historical studies.

Such a conclusion is at one and the same time cautious and yet so broad as to seem banal. If it is disappointing it is, unfortunately, a reflection of the theoretical state of the art. We might be methodologically more sophisticated and cautious than we were a decade ago, but we are as far as ever from developing an integrated theory of development and/or underdevelopment.

NOTES

1. I ask the reader to take these terms unquestioned at the moment. It is the intention of this monograph to demonstrate both their utility and inadequacy.

2. Generally on these very broad issues in contemporary social and political theory see Bock 1978; Bury 1928; Pollard 1968; Nisbet 1968 and 1980.

3. Frey (1978) points to three major streams: first, Marxian political economy (strongly influenced by Ricardo); second, non-economic approaches based on systems theory, systems analysis and policy science; third, a political economy with its origins in modern economic theory. On the burgeoning body of political economy literature, both radical and orthodox, see Frey 1978, Leaver 1978, Walleri 1978, Cox 1979 and Garson 1978: Ch. 6.

4. See especially Parsons' basic statement on pattern variables in *The Social System* (1951). Its application to developing societies is best expressed in Hoselitz 1960. Of the numerous critiques of the supposed exclusivity of tradition and modernity see Tipps 1973, Bernstein 1971 and Frank 1971.

5. Lasswell's work was, of course, of paramount importance in the foundation of a policy-based political science. His approach sought the answers that problem-oriented research could provide to the following questions: What goal values are to be sought? What are the trends in the realisation of values? What factors condition trends? What projections characterise the probable course of future developments? What policy alternative will bring the greatest net realisation of values? (Lasswell, 1958: 187); but see also Lasswell 1971. For a discussion of Lasswell, see Brewer and Brunner 1975.

6. Bienan (1971) has applied a machine analogy to contemporary African party political activity and Roth (1968) and Willame (1972) have argued that Weber's ideas about patrimonialism are more useful than his ideas relating to charisma when it comes to talking about authority in Africa.

7. There is also a reasonable body of literature in the area of development administration which we might call 'the British School', which includes Bernard Schaffer. Work from within this school does not, however, appear to have had a great deal of influence on North American political science.

8. A content analysis of 'Radical Readers' on underdevelopment during the early 1970s would reveal the extent of the influence of Frank's work during that period. For the 'essential Frank' see his works of 1966, 1969a and 1972, from which my discussion is largely taken.

9. By far the most comprehensive review of varieties of Latin American dependency theory to date is Di Palma 1978.

10. For a discussion of the debate between Lenin and Luxemburg see Cohen 1975.

11. For an excellent review of the 'sucking out of surplus debate' see Mack and Leaver 1979.

12. Wallerstein's major work to date is his *Modern World System*, vol. I (1974), a detailed discussion of the origins of the European world economy in the sixteenth century. His basic theoretical statements are to be found in a series of articles, especially 1975, 1974a, 1974b. These have been collected together in *The Capitalist World Economy* (1978).

13. See particularly the comments by Charles Bettelheim reproduced as an appendix to Emmanuel's own *Unequal Exchange* (1972). For an excellent review of Emmanuel, see Mack 1974.

14. Examples of work operating in a Wallersteinian mould are to be found in Chirot 1977, Chase-Dunn and Rubinson 1977, and Hockey-Kaplan 1978. For a critique, see Gerstein 1977.

15. The work of these anthropologists is collected together in Seddon 1978 and discussed in Clammer 1979; see also the collection of essays on the articulation of modes of production in Wolpe 1979.

16. For example, Alavi (1975 and 1979) talks about the colonial mode as well as the feudalist and capitalist modes of production. Amin (1974b and 1976) talks about peasant modes. Foster-Carter (1978) and Bernstein (1979: 87-9) provide good discussions of this proliferation.

17. Some authors seem to think that the answer has to be an emphatic 'Yes'. See Hirschmann 1981 — note this is not Albert O. Hirschmann.

18. It is interesting to note that the first ever meeting of the American Political Science Association to be devoted to a single theme took place in New York in 1981 to discuss 'Bringing the State Back Into Political Science'!

19. For introductory guides see Nawaz 1980 and Cox 1979.

REFERENCES

Ake, C. (1976) 'Explanatory Notes on the Political Economy of Africa', *Journal of Modern African Studies*, *14* (1): 1-4.
Alavi, H. (1979) 'The Structure of Colonial Social Formations', *Underdevelopment – an International Comparison*, University of Bielefield, mimeo.
— (1975) 'India, and the Colonial Mode of Production' in R. Miliband and J. Saville (eds.), *Socialist Register*: 160-97
— (1972) 'The State in Post-Colonial Societies: Pakistan and Bangladesh', *New Left Review*, *74*: 59-81
Almond, G. A. (1970) *Political Development: Essays in Heuristic Theory*, Little, Brown, Boston
— (1966) 'Political Theory and Political Science', *American Political Science Review*, *60* (4): 869-79
— and Coleman, J. (eds.) (1960) *The Politics of Developing Areas*, Princeton University Press, Princeton
—, Mundt, R. A., and Flanagan, C. (eds.) (1973) *Crisis, Choice and Change: Historical Studies of Political Development*, Little, Brown, Boston
— and Genco, S. (1977) 'Clouds, Clocks and the Study of Politics', *World Politics*, *29* (4): 489-522
— and Powell, B. J. (1978) *Comparative Politics: System, Process and Policy*, Little, Brown, Boston
—, — (1966) *Comparative Politics: a Developmental Approach*, Little, Brown, Boston
— and Verba, S. (1963) *The Civic Culture*, Little, Brown, Boston
Amin, S. (1978) *Imperialism and Unequal Development*, Harvester Press, Sussex
— (1976) *Unequal Development: an Essay on the Social Formation of Peripheral Capitalism*, Harvester Press, Sussex
— (1976a) 'Self-reliance and the New International Economic Order', *Monthly Review*, *29* (3): 1-21
— (1974) *Accumulation on a World Scale*, 2 vols., Monthly Review Press, New York
— (1974a) 'Accumulation and Development: a Theoretical Model', *Review of African Political Economy 1* (August-November): 9-26
— (1973) *Neo-Colonialism in West Africa*, Penguin, Harmondsworth
— (1972) 'Underdevelopment and Dependence in Black Africa – Origins and Contemporary Forms', *Journal of Modern African Studies*, *10* (4): 503-24
Anderson, C. W. (1975) 'System and Strategy in Comparative Policy Analysis: a Plea for Contextual and Experiential Knowledge' in B. W. Gwyn and G. C. Edwards (eds.), *Perspectives on Policy-Making*, Studies in Political Science, Tulane
Apter, D. (1980) 'The Passing of Development Studies: Over the Shoulder with a Backward Glance', *Government and Opposition*, *15* (3/4): 263-75
— (1971) *Choice and the Politics of Allocation*, Yale University Press, New Haven
— (1965) *The Politics of Modernisation*, Chicago University Press, Chicago
— (1957) *Ghana in Transition*, Princeton University Press, Princeton
Arrighi, G. (1978) *The Geometry of Imperialism*, New Left Books, London
Avineri, S. (1969) *Karl Marx on Colonialism and Modernisation*, Anchor Books, New York
Bachrach, P., and Baratz, M. S. (1970) *Power and Poverty: Theory and Practice*,

Oxford University Press, London

Ball, T. (1976) 'From Paradigms to Research Programs: Towards a Post Kuhnian Political Science', *American Journal of Political Science*, *20* (1): 151-77

Baran, P. (1957) *The Political Economy of Growth*, Monthly Review Press, New York

Barker, J. (1981) 'Beyond the Peasant Principle: the State and the Art of Political Economy in Rural Africa' in P. Ray, P. Shinnie and D. Williams, *Into the 1980s: Proceedings of the Eleventh Annual Conference of the Canadian African Studies Association*, Tantalus, Vancouver

Barratt-Brown, M. (1970) *After Imperialism*, Heinemann, London

Barry, B. (1977) 'Crisis, Choice and Change', *British Journal of Political Science*, *7* (1): 217-53

Bates, R. (1981) *Markets and States in Africa*, University of California Press, Berkeley

Bauer, P. (1981) *Equality, the Third World and Economic Delusion*, Harvard University Press, Cambridge, Mass.

— (1976) *Dissent of Development*, Heinemann, London

Bendix, R. (1967) 'Tradition and Modernity Reconsidered', *Comparative Studies in Society and History*, *9* (3): 292-346

Berger, P. (1976) *Pyramids of Sacrifice: Political Ethics and Social Change*, Allen Lane, London

Bergsten, C. F., and Krause, L. B. (eds.) (1975) *World Politics and International Economics*, Brookings Institution, Washington, DC

Berman, B. J. (1978) 'Letter to the Editor', *American Political Science Review*, *72* (2): 207-9

— (1974) 'Clientalism and Neo-colonialism: Centre Periphery Relations and Political Development in African States', *Studies in Comparative International Development*, *9* (1): 3-25

Bernstein, H. (1979) 'Sociology of Development versus Sociology of Underdevelopment?' in D. Lehmann (ed.), *Development Theory: Four Critical Studies*, Cass, London

— (1971) 'Modernisation Theory and the Sociological Study of Development', *Journal of Development Studies*, *7* (2): 141-60

Bettleheim, C. (1972) 'A Reply to Emmanuel' in A. Emmanuel, *Unequal Exchange: a Study of the Imperialism of Trade*, New Left Books, London

Bienen, H. (1971) 'Political Parties and Political Machines' in M. Lofchie (ed.), *The State of the Nations: Constraints on Development in Independent Africa*, University of California Press, Berkeley

Binder, L., Pye, L. W., Coleman, J. S., Verba, S., LaPalombara, J., and Weiner, M. (1971) *Crises and Sequences in Political Development*, Princeton University Press, Princeton

Black, C. E. (1967) *The Dynamics of Modernisation*, Harper Row, New York

Blondel, J. (1978) *Thinking Politically*, Penguin, Harmondsworth

Bock, K. (1978) 'Theories of Progress, Development and Evolution' in T. Bottomore and R. Nisbet (eds.), *A History of Sociological Analysis*, Heinemann, London

Bodenheimer, S. J. (1971) *The Ideology of Developmentalism: the American Paradigm – Surrogate for Latin American Studies*, Sage, Beverly Hills

Boulding, K. (1965) *The Meaning of the Twentieth Century*, Harper Colophon, New York

Brandt, W. *et al*. (1980) *North-South: a Programme for Survival*, Pan, London

Brenner, R. (1977) 'The Origins of Capitalist Development: a Critique of Neo-Smithian Marxism', *New Left Review*, *104* (July-August): 25-92

Brewer, A. (1980) *Marxist Theories of Imperialism: a Critical Perspective*,

Routledge and Kegan Paul, London

Brewer, D. G., and Brunner, R. D. (eds.) (1975) *Political Development and Change: a Policy Approach* Free Press, New York

Brittain, S. (1975) 'The Economic Contradictions of Democracy', *British Journal of Political Science*, 5 (April): 129-59

Bukharin, N. (1972) *Imperialism and the World Economy*, Merlin Press, London, first published 1917

Bury, J. B. (1928) *The Idea of Progress: an Inquiry into its Origins and Growth*, Macmillan, London

Cabral, A. (1969) *Revolution in Guinea: an African People's Struggle*, Stage One, London

Campbell, B. (1978) 'Ivory Coast' in J. Dunn (ed.), *West African States: Failure and Promise*, Cambridge University Press, London

Caporaso, J. (1978) 'Introduction to the Special Issue International Organisation on Dependence and Dependency in the Global System', *International Organisation*, 32 (1): 1-12

— (1978a) 'Dependence, Dependency, and Power in the Global System: a Structural Analysis', *International Organisation*, 32 (1): 13-29

Cardoso, F. H. (1973) 'Associated Dependent Development: Theoretical and Practical Implications' in A. H. Stepan (ed.), *Authoritarian Brazil*, Yale University Press, New Haven

Cawson, A. (1978) 'Pluralism, Corporatism and the Role of the State', *Government and Opposition*, 131: 178-98

Chase-Dunn, C., and Rubinson, R. (1977) 'Toward a Structural Perspective on the World System', *Politics and Society*, 7 (4): 453-76

Chenery, H. *et al*. (1979) *Structural Change and Development Policy*, Oxford University Press, London

— *et al*. (1974) *Redistribution with Growth*, Oxford University Press, London

Chirot, D. (1977) *Social Change in the Twentieth Century* Harcourt, Brace, Jovanovich, New York

Clammer, J. (ed.) (1979) *The New Economic Anthropology*, Macmillan, London

— (1975) 'Economic Anthropology and the Sociology of Development: Liberal Anthropology and its French critics' in I. Oxaal, T. Barnett and D. Booth, *Beyond the Sociology of Development*, Routledge and Kegan Paul, London

Cohen, B. (1975) *A Question of Imperialism: the Political Economy of Dominance and Dependence*, Macmillan, London

Cohen, R. (1972) 'Class in Africa: Analytical Problems and Perspectives' in R. Miliband and J. Saville (eds.), *Socialist Register*

Coleman, J. (ed.) (1965) *Education and Political Development*, Princeton University Press, Princeton

— (1958) *Nigeria: Background to Nationalism*, University of California Press, Berkeley

— and Rosberg, C. G. (1966) *Political Parties and National Integration in Tropical Africa*, University of California Press, Berkeley

Cooper, F. (1981) 'Africa and the World Economy', African Studies Association, Bloomington, Indiana

Cox, R. (1979) 'Ideologies and the New International Economic Order: Reflections on Some Recent Literature', *International Organisation*, 32 (2): 257-302

Crenson, M. A. (1971) *The Un-politics of Air Pollution: a Study of Non-Decision-Making in the Cities*, The Johns Hopkins Press, Baltimore

Crompton, R., and Gubbay, J. (1977) *Economy and Class Structure*, Macmillan, London

Cumper, G. E. (1973) 'Non-economic Factors Influencing Rural Development Planning' in H. Bernstein (ed.), *Underdevelopment and Development*, Penguin

Harmondsworth

Debray, R. (1967) *Revolution in the Revolution*, Penguin, Harmondsworth

Di Palma, G. (1978) 'Dependency: a Formal Theory of Underdevelopment or a Methodology for the Analysis of Concrete Situations of Underdevelopment?' *World Development*, 6: 881-924

Dos Santos, T. (1973) 'The Structure of Dependence' in C. K. Wilber (ed.), *The Political Economy of Development and Underdevelopment*, Random House, New York

Dror, Y. (1968) *Public Policy-Making Reexamined*, Chandler Publishing, Pennsylvania

Dupuy, A., and Fitzgerald, P. V. (1977) 'A Contribution to the Critique of the World System Perspective', *Insurgent Sociologist*, 7 (2): 113-23

Duvall, R. (1978) 'Dependence and Dependencia Theory: Notes Towards Precision of Concept and Argument', *International Organisation*, 32 (1): 51-78

— and Freeman, J. (1981) 'The State and Dependent Capitalism', *International Studies Quarterly*, 25 (1): 99-118

Easton, D. (1969) 'The New Revolution in Political Science', *American Political Science Review*, 62 (4): 1051-61

Ehrensaft, P. (1971) 'Semi-industrial Capitalism: the Implications for Social Research in Africa', *Africa Today*, 18: 40-67

Eisenstadt, S. (1973) *Tradition, Change and Modernity*, John Wiley, New York

— (1966) *Modernisation: Protest and Change*, Prentice-Hall, Englewood Cliffs

Elkin, S. (1974) 'Political Science and the Analysis of Public Policy', *Public Policy*, 22: 319-422

Emmanuel, A. (1976) 'The Multinational Corporations and Inequality of Development', *International Social Science Journal*, 28 (4): 754-72

— (1974) 'Myths of Development versus Myths of Underdevelopment', *New Left Review*, 85 (May-June): 61-81

— (1972) *Unequal Exchange: a Study of the Imperialism of Trade*, New Left Books, London

Evans, P. (1979) *Dependent Development: the Alliance of Multinational, State and Local Capital in Brazil*, Princeton University Press, Princeton

Falk, R. (1979) 'A World Order Perspective on Authoritarian Tendencies', *Alternatives*, 5 (1): 127-93

Feldman, E. J. (1978) 'Comparative Public Policy', *Comparative Politics*, 10 (2): 287-305

First, R. (1971) *The Barrel of a Gun*, Allen Lane, London

Foster-Carter, A. (1980) 'Marxism and Dependency Theory: a Polemic', *Millennium*, 8 (3): 214-34

— (1978) 'The Modes of Production Controversy', *New Left Review*, 107 (January-February): 47-77

— (1976) 'From Rostow to Gunder Frank: Conflicting Paradigms in the Analysis of Underdevelopment', *World Development*, 4 (3): 167-80

— (1974) 'Neo-Marxist Approaches to Development and Underdevelopment' in E. de Kadt and G. Williams (eds.), *Sociology and Development*, Tavistock Publications, London

Frank, A. G. (1972) *Lumpenbourgeoisie, Lumpendevelopment*, Monthly Review Press, New York

— (1971) *The Sociology of Development and the Underdevelopment of Sociology*, Pluto Press, London

— (1969) *Capitalism and Underdevelopment in Latin America*, Monthly Review Press, New York

— (1969a) *Latin America: Underdevelopment or Revolution*, Monthly Review Press, New York

— (1966) 'The Development of Underdevelopment', *Monthly Review*, *18* (4), reprinted in Frank 1969a

Frankel, B. (1978) *Marxian Theories of the State: a Critique of Orthodoxy*, Arena Publications, Melbourne

Frey, B. S. (1978) *Modern Political Economy*, Martin Robertson, London

Galtung, J. (1971) 'A Structural Theory of Imperialism', *Journal of Peace Research*, *13* (2): 81-121

Garson, D. G. (1978) *Group Theories of Politics*, Sage, London

Gerstein, I. (1977) 'Theories of the World Economy and Imperialism', *Insurgent Sociologist*, *7* (2): 9-22

George, S. (1976) *How the Other Half Dies*, Penguin, Harmondsworth

Godelier, M. (1977) *Perspectives in Marxist Anthropology*, Cambridge University Press, Cambridge

Godfrey, M. (ed.) (1980) 'Is Dependency Dead?' *Bulletin of the Institute of Development Studies, Sussex*, *12* (1)

Goldsworthy, D. (n.d.) 'Analysing Theories of Development', Monash University, mimeo.

Goulbourne, H. (ed.) (1979) *Politics and the State in the Third World*, Macmillan, London

Gouldner, A. W. (1970) *The Coming Crisis of Western Sociology*, Heinemann, London

Goulet, D. (1976) 'On the Ethics of Development Planning', *Studies in Comparative International Development*, *11* (1): 25-43

Grew, R. (1980) 'More on Modernisation', *Journal of Social History*, *14* (2): 1-15

Griffin, K. (1969) *Underdevelopment in Spanish America*, Allen and Unwin, London

Grindle, M. (1981) 'Anticipating Failures: the Implementation of Rural Development Programs', *Public Policy*, *29* (1): 51-74

— (ed.) (1980) *Politics and Policy Implementation in the Third World*, Princeton University Press, Princeton

Guevara, C. (1969) *Guerilla War*, Penguin, London

Gusfield, J. R. (1967) 'Tradition and Modernity: Misplaced Polarities in the Study of Social Change', *American Journal of Sociology*, *72* (January): 351-62

Habermas, J. (1976) *Legitimation Crisis*, Heinemann, London

Hagen, E. (1962) *On the Theory of Social Change*, Dorsey Press, Illinois

Halpern, M. (1965) 'The Rate and Costs of Political Development', *Annals of the American Academy of Political Science*, *382* (March): 20-8

Harries, O. (1979) 'The Ideology of the Third World' in *Australia and the Third World: Report of the Committee on Australia's Relations with the Third World*, AGPS, Canberra, Appendix U

Hartz, L. (1955) *The Liberal Tradition in America: an Interpretation of American Political Thought Since the Revolution*, Harcourt, Brace, New York

Hayter, T. (1971) *Aid as Imperialism*, Penguin, Harmondsworth

Heclo, H. (1972) 'Policy Analysis', *British Journal of Political Science*, *2* (1): 85-107

Higgott, R. (1983) 'The State of the Art on the Art of the State: Some Thoughts on the Future Drawn From the Past' in T. Shaw (ed.), *Africa Projected: from Dependence to Self Reliance by the Year 2000?* Macmillan, London, forthcoming

— (1980) 'Structural Dependence and Decolonisation in a West African Land-Locked State: the Case of Niger', *Review of African Political Economy*, *17* (July-August): 43-58

— (1978) 'Competing Theoretical Perspectives on Development and Under-

2222
2222
2222

2222
2222

2

development: a Recent Intellectual History', *Politics, 13* (1): 26-41

Higgott and Robison, R. (eds.) 1983 *Southeast Asia: Essays in the Political Economy of Structural Change*, Routledge and Kegal Paul, London, forthcoming

Hilferding, R. (1923) *Finance Capital*, Vorwers, Vienna, first published 1910

Hirsch, F. (1977) *The Social Limits to Growth*, Routledge and Kegan Paul, London

Hirschman, A. O. (1978) 'Beyond Asymmetry: Critical Notes on Myself as a Young Man and on Some Other Old Friends', *International Organisation, 32* (1): 45-9

— (1975) 'Policy Making and Policy Analysis in Latin America: a Return Journey', *Policy Science, 6* (4): 385-402

— (1970) *Exist, Voice and Loyalty: Responses to Decline in Firms, Organisations and States*, Harvard University Press, Cambridge, Mass.

— (1945) *National Power and the Structure of Foreign Trade*, University of California Press, Berkeley

Hirschman, D. (1981) 'Development or Underdevelopment Administration', *Development and Change, 12* (3): 459-79

Hobson, J. A. (1965) *Imperialism – a Study*, Michigan University Press, Michigan, first published 1902

Hockey-Kaplan, B. (ed.) (1978) *Social Change in the Capitalist World Economy*, Sage, Beverly Hills

Holt, R. T., and Turner, J. E. (1975) 'Crises and Sequences in Collective Development Theory', *American Political Science Review, 64* (3): 979-94

Hopkins, A. G. (1976) 'Clio-Antics: a Horoscope for African Economic History' in C. Fyfe (ed.), *African Studies Since 1945: a Tribute to Basil Davidson*, Longmans, London

— (1975) 'On Importing André Gunder Frank into Africa', *African Economic History Review, 2* (1): 13-21

Huntington, S. P. (1968) *Political Order in Changing Societies*, Yale University Press, New Haven

— (1965) 'Political Development and Political Decay', *World Politics, 17* (3): 386-430

— *et al.* (1975) *The Crisis of Democracy*, Columbia University Press, New York

Hyden, G. (1980) *Beyond Ujaama in Tanzania: Underdevelopment and an Uncaptured Peasantry*, Heinemann, London

Illchman, W., and Uphoff, N. T. (1969) *The Political Economy of Change*, University of California Press, Los Angeles

Jalée, P. (1968) *The Pillage of the Third World*, Monthly Review Press, New York

Jenkins, W. I. (1978) *Policy Analysis: a Political and Organisational Perspective*, Martin Robertson, London

Kaufman, R. *et al.* (1975) 'A Preliminary Test of the Theory of Dependency', *Comparative Politics, 7* (3): 303-30

Kay, G. (1975) *Development and Underdevelopment: a Marxist Analysis*, Macmillan, London

Keohane, R. O., and Nye, J. S. (1976) 'International Economics and International Politics: a Framework for Analysis' in O. Blake and R. S. Walters, *The Politics of Global Economic Relations*, Prentice-Hall, Englewood Cliffs

— (1973) *Transnational Relations and World Politics*, Harvard University Press, Cambridge, Mass.

Kesselman, M. (1973) 'Order or Movement: the Literature of Political Development as Ideology', *World Politics, 26* (1): 139-54

Kiernan, V. G. (1974) *Marxism and Imperialism*, Edward Arnold, London
Killick, A. (1980) 'Trends in Development Economics and their Relevance to Africa', *Journal of Modern African Studies*, *18* (3): 367-86
Kindleberger, C. (1958) *Economic Development*, McGraw Hill, London
Kon, I. S. (1975) 'The Crisis of Western Sociology and the "Second Discovery" of Marxism' in T. Bottomore (ed.), *Crisis and Contention in Sociology*, Sage, Beverly Hills
Kothari, R. (1968) 'Tradition and Modernity Revisited', *Government and Opposition*, *3* (2): 273-93
Kuhn, T. (1978) *The Essential Tension: Selected Studies in Scientific Tradition and Change*, Chicago University Press, Chicago
— (1962) *The Structure of Scientific Revolutions*, 2nd edn, Chicago University Press, Chicago
Laclau, E. (1975) 'The Specificity of the Political: Around the Poulantzas-Miliband Debate', *Economy and Society*, *4* (1): 87-110
— (1971) 'Imperialism in Latin America', *New Left Review*, *67*: 19-38
Lall, S. (1975) 'Is "Dependence" a Useful Concept in Analysing Underdevelopment?' *World Development*, *3*: 799-810
Lakatos, I. and Musgrave, A. (eds.) (1970) *Criticism and the Growth of Knowledge*, Cambridge University Press, London
LaPalombara, J. (ed.) (1963) *Bureaucracy and Political Development*, Princeton University Press, Princeton
— and Weiner, M. (eds.) (1966) *Political Parties and Political Development*, Princeton University Press, Princeton
Lasswell, H. D. (1971) *A Pre-View of Policy Sciences*, Elsevier, New York
— (1958) *Politics, Who Gets What, When, How*, Meridan, Cleveland
Law, R. (1978) 'In Search of a Marxist Perspective on Pre-Colonial Tropical Africa', *Journal of African History*, *19* (3): 441-52
Leaver, R. (1979) *Amin on Underdevelopment*, Flinders University, South Australia, mimeo.
— (1978) *Towards the Political Economy of International Relations: the End of the World as We Know it?* Department of International Relations, Australian National University, Canberra, mimeo.
Lehmann, D. (ed.) (1979) *Development Theory: Four Critical Studies*, Cass, London
— (1974) *Peasants, Landlords and Governments*, Holmes and Meier, New York
Leichtheim, G. (1963) 'Marx and the Asiatic Mode of Production', *St. Anthony's Papers*, *14*
Lenin, V. I. (1970) *Imperialism, the Highest Stage of Capitalism*, Progress Publishers, Moscow, first published 1917
Leys, C. (1978) 'Capital Accumulation, Class Formation and Dependency – the Significance of the Kenyan Case', *Socialist Register*: 241-66
— (1977) 'Underdevelopment and Dependency: Critical Notes', *Journal of Contemporary Asia*, 7 (1): 92-107
— (1976) 'The "Over-Developed" Post-Colonial State: a Re-evaluation', *Review of African Political Economy*, *5* (January-April): 39-48
— (1974) *Underdevelopment in Kenya: the Political Economy of Colonialism*, Heinemann, London
— and Borges, J. (1979) 'State Capitalism in Kenya', Canadian Political Studies Association (June)
Lindblom, C. E. (1959) 'The Science of Muddling Through', *Public Administration Review*, *19* (2): 79-88
Lipton, M. (1977) *Why People Stay Poor: Urban Bias in World Development*, Temple Smith, London

Lofchie, M. (1981) 'Africa and the World Economy', African Studies Association, Bloomington, Indiana

Long, N. (1977) *An Introduction to the Sociology of Rural Development*, Tavistock Publications, London

Love, J. (1980) 'Raúl Prebish and the Doctrine of Unequal Exchange', *Latin American Research Review, 15* (November): 45-72

Lowi, T. (1970) 'Decision Making in Public Policy', *Public Administration Review, 30* (4): 314-25

Lukes, S. (1974) *Power: a Radical View*, Macmillan, London

Luton, H. (1976) 'The Satellite-Metropolis Model: a Critique', *Theory and Society, 3* (4)

Luxemburg, R. (1951) *The Accumulation of Capital*, Routledge and Kegan Paul, London, first published 1913

Mack, A. (1974) 'Theories of Imperialism: the European Perspective', *Journal of Conflict Resolution, 18*: 514-35

— and Leaver, R. (1979) 'Radical Theories of Underdevelopment: an Assessment' in A. Mack, R. Doyle and D. Plant (eds.), *Imperialism, Intervention and Development*, Croom Helm, London

Magdoff, H. (1969) *The Age of Imperialism*, Monthly Review Press, New York

Meadows, D. *et al.* (1972) *The Limits to Growth*, Pan Books, London

Meillassoux, C. (1972) 'From Reproduction to Production: a Marxist Approach to Economic Anthropology', *Economy and Society, 1* (1)

Migdal, J. S. (1977) 'Policy and Power: a Framework for the Study of Comparative Policy Contexts in Third World Countries', *Public Policy, 25* (2): 241-60

— (1974) *Peasants, Politics and Revolution in the Third World*, Princeton University Press, Princeton

Miliband, R. (1977) *Marxism and Politics*, Oxford University Press, London

— (1970) 'The Capitalist State: a Reply to Nicos Poulantzas', *New Left Review, 59*: 53-60

Milne, R. S. (1972) 'The Overdeveloped Study of Political Development', *Canadian Journal of Political Science, 5* (4): 560-8

— (1972a) 'Decision-making in Developing Countries', *Journal of Comparative Administration, 3* (4): 397-405

Mitchell, W. C. (1969) 'The Shape of Political Theory to Come: from Political Sociology to Political Economy' in S. M. Lipset (ed.), *Politics and the Social Sciences*, Oxford University Press, London

Mohri, K. (1979) 'Marx and Underdevelopment', *Monthly Review, 30* (11): 32-42

Montgomery, J. (1969) 'The Quest for Political Development', *Comparative Politics, 1* (2): 285-95

Mouzelis, N. (1980) 'Modernisation, Underdevelopment, Uneven Development: Prospects for a Theory of Third World Formations', *Journal of Peasant Studies, 7* (3): 353-74

Myrdal, G. (1972) *Economic Theory and Underdeveloped Regions*, Methuen, London

McClelland, D. (1961) *The Achieving Society*, Van Nostrand, New Jersey

McFarlane, B. (1978) *Theories of Imperialism: Political Aspects*, Australian Political Studies Association, Adelaide, 18pp.

McGowan, P. (1976) 'Economic Development and Economic Performance in Black Africa', *Journal of Modern African Studies, 14* (10): 25-40

— and Smith, D. L. (1978) 'Economic Dependency in Black Africa: an Analysis of Competing Theories', *International Organisation, 32* (1): 179-235

McHenry, D. (1979) *Tanzania's Ujaama Villages: the Implementation of Rural*

Development Strategy, Institute of International Studies, Berkeley

McMichael, P., Petras, J., and Rhodes, R. (1974) 'Imperialism and the Contradictions of Capitalism', *New Left Review*, *85* (May-June): 84-104

Nafziger, W. (1979) 'A Critique of Development Economics in the U.S.' in D. Lehmann (ed.), *Development Theory: Four Critical Studies*, Cass, London

Nawaz, T. (1980) *The New International Economic Order: a Bibliography*, Westwood Press, Connecticut

Nisbet, R. (1980) *History of the Idea of Progress*, Basic Books, New York

— (1968) *Social Change and History*, Free Press, New York

Nordlinger, E. (1981) *On the Autonomy of the Modern Democratic State*, Harvard University Press, Cambridge Mass.

Nove, A. (1974) 'On Reading André Gunder Frank', *Journal of Development Studies*, *10* (3/4): 445-55

Nye, R. A. (1976-7) 'The Anti-Democratic Sources of Elite Theory: Pareto, Mosca, Michels', *Comparative Political Sociology*, *2*: 5-57

O'Brien, D. C. (1972) 'Modernisation, Order and the Erosion of a Democratic Ideal: American Political Science 1960-1970', *Journal of Development Studies*, *8* (2): 351-78

O'Brien, P. (1975) 'A Critique of Latin American Theories of Dependency' in I. Oxaal, T. Barnett and D. Booth (eds.), *Beyond the Sociology of Development*, Routledge and Kegan Paul, London

O'Connor, J. (1973) *The Fiscal Crisis of the State*, St. Martins Press, New York

— (1970) 'The Meaning of Economic Imperialism' in R. I. Rhodes (ed.), *Imperialism and Underdevelopment*, Monthly Review Press, New York

Owen, R. and Sutcliffe, B. (eds.) (1972) *Studies in the Theory of Imperialism*, Longman, London

Oxaal, I., Barnett, T., and Booth, D. (1975) *Beyond the Sociology of Development*, Routledge and Kegan Paul, London

Packenham, R. A. (1973) *Liberal America and the Third World: Political Development Ideas in Foreign Aid and Social Science*, Princeton University Press, Princeton

Panitch, L. (1980) 'Recent Theorisations of Corporatism: Reflections on a Growth Industry', *British Journal of Sociology*, *31* (2): 159-87

— (1977) 'The Development of Corporatism in Liberal Democracies', *Comparative Political Studies*, *10* (1): 61-90

Parsons, T. (1951) *The Social System*, Routledge and Kegan Paul, London

Perry, N. (1977) 'A Comparative Analysis of Paradigm Proliferation', *British Journal of Sociology*, *28*: 38-50

Peters, B. G. (1979) 'Bureaucracy, Politics and Public Policy', *Comparative Politics*, *11* (3): 339-58

Petras, J. (1975) 'New Perspectives on Social Imperialism: Social Classes in the Periphery', *Journal of Contemporary Asia*, *5* (3): 291-308

— and Trachte, K. (1978) 'Liberal, Structural and Radical Approaches to Political Economy: an Assessment' in J. Petras, *Critical Perspectives on Imperialism and Social Class in the Third World*, Monthly Review Press, New York

Phillips, A. (1977) 'The Concept of Development', *Review of African Political Economy*, *8* (January-April): 7-20

Pool, I. de Sola (ed.) (1967) *Contemporary Political Science: Towards Empirical Theory*, McGraw Hill, New York

Poulantzas, N. (1969) 'The Problem of the Capitalist State', *New Left Review*, *58*: 67-78

Pratt, R. P. (1973) 'The Underdeveloped Political Science of Political Development', *Studies in Comparative International Development*, *8* (1): 88-112

Prebisch, R. (1963) *Towards a Dynamic Development Policy in Latin America*,

United Nations, New York
— (1950) *The Economic Development of Latin America and its Principal Problems*, United Nations, New York
Price, R. (1975) *Bureaucracy and Society in Contemporary Ghana*, University of California Press, Berkeley
Pye, L. (1966) *Aspects of Political Development*, Little, Brown, Boston
— (ed.) (1963) *Communication and Political Development*, Princeton University Press, Princeton
— (1962) *Politics, Personality and Nation Building: Burma's Search for Identity*, Yale University Press, New Haven
— and Verba, S. (eds.) (1965) *Political Culture and Political Development*, Princeton University Press, Princeton
Ray, D. (1973) 'The Dependency Model of Latin American Underdevelopment: Three Basic Fallacies', *Journal of Inter-American Studies and World Affairs*, *15*: 4-20
Ricci, D. (1977) 'Reading Thomas Kuhn in the Post-Behavioural Era', *Western Political Quarterly*, *77* (March): 7-34
Robinson, J. (1976) *Economic Philosophy*, Penguin, Harmondsworth
Rodney, W. (1972) *How Europe Underdeveloped Africa*, Bogel Ouverture, London
Rogowski, R. (1978) 'Rationalist Theories of Politics: a Mid-Term Report', *World Politics*, *30* (2): 296-323
Rosberg, C. (1963) 'Democracy in the New Africa', *St. Anthony's Papers*, *15* (2)
Rose, R. (1973) 'Comparing Public Policy: an Overview', *European Journal of Political Research*, *1* (1): 67-94
— and Peters, B. G. (1977) *Can Governments Go Bankrupt?* Basic Books, New York
Rosenau, J. (1971) *The Scientific Study of Foreign Policy*, Free Press, New York
Rostow, W. (1960) *Politics and the Stages of Growth*, Cambridge University Press, Cambridge
Roth, G. (1968) 'Personal Rulership, Patrimonialism and Empire Building in New States', *World Politics*, *20* (2): 194-206
Rothchild, D., and Curry, R. L. (1978) *Scarcity, Choice and Public Policy in Middle Africa*, University of California Press, Berkeley
Rothstein, R. L. (1977) *The Weak in the World of the Strong: the Developing Countries in the International System*, Columbia University Press, New York
Roxborough, I. (1979) *Theories of Underdevelopment*, Macmillan, London
— (1976) 'Dependency Theory in the Sociology of Development: Some Theoretical Problems', *West African Journal of Sociology and Political Science*, *1* (2): 11-133
Russell, C., and Nicholson, N. (1981) *Public Choice and Rural Development*, Resources for the Future, Washington, DC
Sandbrook, R. (1976) 'The Crisis in Political Development Theory', *Journal of Development Studies*, *12* (2): 165-85
Sartori, G. (1970) 'Concept Misinformation in Comparative Politics', *American Political Science Review*, *64*
Saul, J. (1974) 'The State in Post-Colonial Societies: Tanzania', *Socialist Register*: 349-72
Scarrow, H. A. (1969) *Comparative Political Analysis*, Harper Row, New York
Schaffer, B. (1978) 'Administrative Legacies and Links in the Post-Colonial State: Preparation, Training and Administrative Reform', *Development and Change*, *9* (2)
Schmitter, P. C. (1974) 'Still the Century of Corporation?', *Review of Politics*, *36* (1), 85-131

Schumacher, E. F. (1975) *Politics, Bureaucracy and Rural Development in Senegal*, University of California Press, Berkeley
— (1974) *Small is Beautiful: a Study of Economics as if People Mattered*, Abacus, London
Scott, J. C. (1976) *The Moral Economy of the Peasant*, Yale University Press, New Haven
Seddon, D. (ed.) (1978) *Relations of Production: Marxist Approaches to Economic Anthropology*, Cass, London
Seers, D. (1979) 'The Birth, Life and Death of Development Economics', *Development and Change*, *10* (4): 707-19
— (1972) 'What are we Trying to Measure', *Journal of Development Studies*, *8* (3): 21-36
Shivji, I. (1976) *Class Struggles in Tanzania*, Heinemann, London
Sklar, H. (ed.) (1980) *Trilateralism*, Southend Press, Boston
Sklar, R. (1981) 'A Response to John Lonsdale's "The State and Social Processes in Africa" ', African Studies Association, Bloomington, Indiana
— (1979) 'The Nature of Class Domination in Africa', *Journal of Modern African Studies*, *17* (4): 531-52
Smith, A. D. (1976) *The Concept of Social Change: A Critique of the Functionalist Theory of Social Change*, Routledge and Kegan Paul, London
Smith, R. F. I. (1977) 'Public Policy and Political Choice: a Review Article', *Australian Journal of Public Administration*, *36* (3): 258-73
Smith, R. B. (1973) 'The Study of Policy-Making in Developing Nations', *Policy Studies Journal*, *9* (4): 244-9
Smith, T. (1979) 'The Underdevelopment of Development Literature: the Case of Dependency Theory', *World Politics*, *31* (2): 247-88
Spero, J. E. (1978) *The Politics of International Economic Relations*, Allen and Unwin, London
Stepan, A. (1978) *The State and Society: Peru in Comparative Perspective*, Princeton University Press, Princeton
Streeton, P. (1980) 'Development Ideas in Historical Perspective', *Regional Development Digest*, *1* (2): 1-34
— (1974) *The Frontiers of Development Studies*, University of London Press, London
Sutcliffe, B. (1972) 'Imperialism and Industrialisation in the Third World' in R. Owen and B. Sutcliffe (eds.), *Studies in the Theory of Imperialism*, Longman, London
Sutcliffe, R. (1971) *Industry and Underdevelopment*, Addison-Wesley, London
Swainson, N. (1979) *The Development of Corporate Capitalism in Kenya: 1918-1978*, Heinemann, London
— (1977) 'The Rise of a National Bourgeoisie in Kenya', *Review of African Political Economy, 8*: 39-55
Taylor, J. (1979) *From Modernisation Theory to Modes of Production: a Critique of the Sociology of Development*, Macmillan, London
— (1974) 'Neo-marxism and Underdevelopment: a Sociological Fantasy', *Journal of Contemporary Asia*, *4* (1): 5-23
Terray, E. (1972) *Marxism and Primitive Societies*, Monthly Review Press, New York
Tinbergen, J. (1976) *Reshaping the International Order: a Report to the Club of Rome*, Dutton, New York
Tipps, D. (1973) 'Modernisation and the Comparative Study of Societies', *Comparative Studies in Society and History*, *15*, 199-226
Trimberger, E. K. (1979) 'World Systems Analysis: the Problem of Unequal Development', *Theory and Society*, *8* (1): 127-37

Tucker, R. (1977) *The Inequality of Nations*, Basic Books, New York
Ul Haq, M. (1976) *The Poverty Curtain: Choices for the Third World*, Columbia University Press, New York
UN/ECLA (1950) *The Economic Development of Latin America and its Principal Problems*, UN/ECLA, New York
Uphoff, N. T., and Illchman, W. (1972) *The Political Economy of Development*, University of California Press, Los Angeles
Wade, L. A. and Curry, R. L. Jr. (1970) *The Logic of Public Policy*, Wadsworth, Belmont, California
Walleri, R. W. (1978) 'The Political Economy Literature of North South Relations', *International Studies Quarterly*, 22 (4): 587-624
Wallerstein, I (1979) *The Capitalist World Economy*, Cambridge University Press, London
— (1978) 'World System Analysis: Theoretical and Interpretative Issues' in B. Hockey-Kaplan (ed.), *Social Change in the Capitalist World Economy*, Sage, Beverly Hills
— (1976) 'From Feudalism to Capitalism: Transition or Transitions', *Social Forces*, 55 (2): 273-83
— (1975) 'Class Formation in the Capitalist World Economy', *Politics and Society*, 5 (3): 367-75
— (1974) *Modern World System: Capitalist Agriculture and the Origins of the European World Economy in the Sixteenth Century*, Academic Press, London
— (1974a) 'Dependence in an Interdependent World: the Limited Possibilities of Transformation within the Capitalist World Economy', *African Studies Review*, 17 (1): 1-26
— (1974b) 'The Rise and Future Demise of the World Capitalist System: Concepts for Comparative Analysis', *Comparative Studies in Society and History*, 16 (4): 387-415
— (1973) 'Class and Class Conflict in Africa', *Canadian Journal of African Studies*, 7 (3): 375-80
Ward, R. E., and Rustow, D. (1964) *Political Modernisation in Japan and Turkey*, Princeton University Press, Princeton
Warren, B. (1980) *Imperialism, Pioneer of Capitalism*, Verso Books, London
— (1973) 'Imperialism and Capitalist Industrialisation', *New Left Review*, 81 (September-October): 3-44
Weiner, M. (1967) *Party Building in a New Nation: the Indian National Congress*, Chicago University Press, Chicago
Willame, J. C. (1972) *Patrimonialism and Political Change in the Congo*, Stanford University Press, Stanford
Winkler, J. T. (1976) 'Corporatism', *Archive Européene de Sociologie*, 17 (1): 100-36
Wolfe, A. (1977) *The Limits of Legitimacy*, Free Press, New York
Wolin, S. (1968) 'Paradigms and Political Theories' in P. King and B. C. Parekh (eds.), *Politics and Experience*, Cambridge University Press, Cambridge, pp. 125-52
Wolpe, H. (ed.) (1979) *The Articulation of Modes of Production: Essays from Economy and Society*, Routledge and Kegan Paul, London
Zolberg, A. (1966) *Creating Political Order: the Party States of West Africa*, Chicago University Press, Chicago

INDEX

academic professionalism 4
accommodation strategies 30-1
accumulation: global 61; process 60
achievement motivation 21
administration 91
administrative power 33
administrative theory 37
Africa 32, 34, 48, 57, 69, 85;
    francophone 70; land-locked
    states 55, 70
African history 41
African socialism 40
African Studies Association 101
aggregation functions 37
agromineral societies 57
ahistoricism 20
aid 35, 56, 100
Ake 34, 67
Alavi 62-3, 67
Almond 15-36 *passim*, 93, 100;
    and Genco 24; and Powell 17, 79;
    and Verba 17; Mundt and
    Flanagan 16, 23
Althusser 60
Althusserian structuralism 62
American liberalism 43; crisis of 9
Amin, Samir 8, 21, 34, 46-67 *passim*,
    75
Anderson 26
Annales School 58
Apter 17-31 *passim*, 40-1, 74-6, 100
Argentina 3
Arrighi 50
Arrow 22
Asia 41, 86
authoritarianism 83, 102; techno-
    cratic 83, 86
Avineri 49

Bachrach 38-9
Ball 7
Ballard viii
Baltimore 38
Bangladesh 3
Baran 8, 21, 46-55, 99
Baratz 38-9
Barratt-Brown 50
Barry 23

Basic Needs 90
Bates 96
Bauer 3, 74, 92-5
behavioural era 17, 23, 26, 42;
    political science 26; theory
    22-4
behaviouralism 5, 14-25
    passim
Bendix 18
Berger 45
Bergsten and Krause 53
Berman 9, 36
Bernstein 14, 20, 64-5, 74-5
Bienen 34
Binder 17-21, 30, 33, 81
Black 1
Blondel 22
Bodenheimer 6, 10, 17
Bodin 9
Boulding 1, 22
bourgeoisie: African 69; bureaucratic
    67-70, 83; comprador 34;
    national 87; pseudo 34; state 70
Brandt Report 91, 95
Braudel 58
Brazil 3, 75, 79, 87
Brazilianisation 83
Brenner 60
Brewer 101
British Free Trade 50
Brugger viii
Bukharin 50
bureaucracy 21, 66; growth 32-3, 83;
    international 98; Third World
    83-4, 96-7
bureaucratic centralisation 32
Burma 17

Cabral 47, 76, 90
Campbell 70
Cancun Conference 91
capital: accumulation 70, 74; African
    69; domestic 69-71; international
    65-9; settler 70
capitalism 48, 55, 100; British in
    India 49; dependent 53, 59;
    Frank's conception 54; global
    58-9, 65; Marx's conception 63;

118

Index

economic theory 23
economy of affection 85
Ehrensaft 48, 55
Eisenstadt 1, 16
elites 34-40 *passim*; African 34; circulation of 86; decision-making 39; dominant 36; first generation 34; maintenance 34-6, 90, 98, 103; national 33; neo-classical 90; policy-making 96-102; political 91; ruling 40, 79; second generation 34; security 41; Third World 34-6; urban 89
Elkin 22
Emmanuel 46, 57-9
equity 41
ethnocentrism 32
Evans 75, 82, 87
evolutionary theorists 16-17
exchange relations 54, 60; global 61; Weberian 60
exemplars 46
export diversification 92
extraction of surplus 56

factor endowments 57
Falk 83
Fanon 47
fascism 16
Feldman 26-7
feudalism 61
First, Ruth 32
Foster-Carter 6, 10, 45-9, 54, 62, 94, 101
Frank 3-14 *passim*, 31, 46-51, 55-61, 67
Frankel 66
function 25, 46

Garson 12
geo-politics 57
George 90
Gertzel viii
Ghana 17
Godelier 62
Godfrey 101
Goldsworthy 76
good society 20
Goulbourne 68
Gouldner xii-xiii, 10, 12, 22, 45
governmental capacity 19, 21
government overload 81
grand theory 17
Grew 8, 103

Griffin 48
Grindle 83
growth 1; without development 55
Guatemala 32
Guevara 47, 86
Gunder Frank *see* Frank
Gusfield 18

Habermas 81
Hagen 21
Halpern 19
Harries 94
Hayter 38
Heclo 26-7
Higgott 14, 70, 82
higher-order values 41
Hilferding 50
Hirschman, Albert 28, 36, 48, 85
historical materialism 54, 102
historiographical analysis vii, 6-8, 99-103
Hobbes xiv, 9
Hobson 50
Hockey Kaplan 58-60
Holt and Turner 15
Hong Kong 75
Hopkins 48-52, 68
human betterment 40-1
Huntington 18-21, 32-4, 81, 95
Hyden xiii, 84, 96-103 *passim*

ideology vii; Liberal 17; of developmentalism 10, 17, 40
Ilchman and Uphoff, 24-8
imperialism 45, 48-51, 58, 68, 103
incrementalism 37-41, 77, 103
India 49
indicative planning 38, 41
industrialisation 51, 55, 56; export promotion 92; import substitution 92; Soviet 99
industrial revolution xii
Institute of Development Studies 90, 92, 101
institutionalisation 15, 21, 32
instrumentalism 41
integration 46
intellectual history vii, xii, 4, 10
interdependence 52
interest articulation 37
international capital *see* capital
international division of labour 59
international dualism 49
international economic order 32

120

Index

Nisbet 95
non-decisions 38-9
non-industrial societies 37
Nordlinger 80-1, 87
normal science 46
normative questions 40
North-South: confrontation 95;
    dialogue 91
Nove 48-9

O'Brien 18-19
O'Connor 50, 81
Olson 22
optimism, post World War II 16, 43
order 18-25, 33-6
organisation theory 97
Oxaal 20, 48

Packenham ix, xiv, 10-17 *passim*,
    43-4, 74
Panitch 81
paradigms 7-10, 42-3, 46
Pareto 86
Parsons 16, 25, 99; pattern variables
    18; value consensus 20
patrimonialism 34
patron-client relations 68
Pearson Report 91
peasants 84-6, 96; immiserisation 86;
    power 85-6; Tanzanian 85-6;
    uncaptured 71
penetrated political system 30
Perry 6
pessimism 21, 36, 41, 43
Peters 83-4
Petras 57, 67
Philippines 75
Phillips 65, 69-70
planning 37-8, 91
Plato 8
pluralism 38-9
policy-analysis 6, 14-15, 21, 26-9,
    35-42, 84
policy implementation 84-6, 93
policy-making: models 36, 90, 98;
    process 2, 26, 35-8, 78-9, 83-4, 93
policy sciences *see* policy studies
policy studies 15, 26-8, 39, 99
political bargaining 37
political behaviour 22
political change xii
political culture 26
political development 14-28 *passim*;
    confused views 19; crises 20;

critiques 20; literature 17-20;
    political science of vii-ix, 12-23
    passim, 42-5, 79; theory 24, 31
political economy 5, 13, 102; attrac-
    tions 12; liberal 12, 92;
    nineteenth century 12; of under-
    development 24-9; *see also* new
    political economy
political instability 81
political order 20; *see also* order and
    modernisation theory
political participation 18-19
political parties 37
political science 17, 21-8 *passim*, 36,
    40-3; American 14, 21, 25, 30;
    behavioural 7, 15, 26, post
    behavioural 14, 19, 43; main-
    stream 80, 99, 102; pluralist 37-8
political socialisation 26
political stability 78
political system 26
politico-administrative power 35
Pool 19, 34, 40
Popper 8, 43
positivism 8, 43, 53
Powell 28-9
pragmatic-pluralist regimes 31
Pratt 20
Prebisch 47-8, 58
pressure groups 37
Price 3
primary produce 61
productionists 54, 62-5, 102
profit repatriation 56
progress xii, 1
proletarian revolution 55; *see also*
    revolution
Poulantzas 60, 66, 80-2
public choice theory 14, 21-7 *passim*,
    76, 96; *see also* rational choice
    theory
public policy of development 15,
    22-44 *passim*, 73, 76, 99
Pye 17-19; and Verba 17

radical: school 45; structuralism 3,
    6, 24, *see also* dependency
    theory; theory 6, 9, 11, 46
Raegan 92
rational choice: models 6, 22-5;
    theory 21-3, 102, *see also* public
    choice theory
rationalists 22
rationality xii